Ben Stacy Jerrik (Ed.)

Copying Mechanism

Ben Stacy Jerrik (Ed.)

Copying Mechanism

Scale-free network, World Wide Web, Preferential attachment

Part Press

Contents

Articles

Copying_mechanism	1
Scale-free_network	3
World_Wide_Web	9
Preferential_attachment	22
Degree_distribution	24
Power_law	26
Probability_distribution	34

References

Article Sources and Contributors	41
Image Sources, Licenses and Contributors	43

Copying_mechanism

In the study of scale-free networks, a **copying mechanism** is a process by which such a network can form and grow, by means of repeated steps in which nodes are duplicated with mutations from existing nodes. Several variations of copying mechanisms have been studied. In the **general copying model**, a growing network starts as a small initial graph and, at each time step, a new vertex is added with a given number k of new outgoing edges. As a result of a stochastic selection, the neighbors of the new vertex are either chosen randomly among the existing vertices, or one existing vertex is randomly selected and k of its neighbors are 'copied' as heads of the new edges.[1]

Motivation

Copying mechanisms for modeling growth of the world wide web are motivated by the following intuition:

- Some web page authors will note an interesting but novel commonality between certain pages, and will link to pages exhibiting this commonality; pages created with this motivation are modeled by a random choice among existing pages.

- Most authors, on the other hand, will be interested in certain already-represented topics, and will collect together links to pages about these topics. Pages created in this way can be modeled by node copying.

Those are the growth and preferential attachment properties of the networks.

Description

For the simple case, nodes are never deleted. At each step we create a new node with a single edge emanating from it. Let u be a page chosen uniformly at random from the pages in existence before this step.

(I) With probability , the only parameter of the model, the new edge points to u.

(II) With probability , the new edge points to the destination of u's (sole) out-link; the new node attains its edge by copying.

The second process increases the probability of high-degree nodes' receiving new incoming edges. In fact, since u is selected randomly, the probability that a webpage with degree will receive a new hyperlink is proportional with , indicating that the copying mechanism effectively amounts to a linear preferential attachment. Kumar et al. prove that the expectation of the incoming degree distribution is , thus follows a power-law with an exponent which varies between 2 (for) and (for).

Above is the linear growth copying model. Since the web is currently growing exponentially, there is the exponential growth copying model. At each step a new epoch of vertices arrives whose size is a constant fraction of the current graph. Each of these vertices may link only to vertices from previous epochs.

The evolving models above are by no means complete. They can be extended in several ways. First of all, the tails in our models were either static, chosen uniformly from the new vertices, or chosen from the existing vertices proportional to their out-degrees. This process could be made more sophisticated to account for the observed deviations of the out-degree distribution from the power-law distribution. Similarly, the models can be extended to include death processes, which cause vertices and edges to disappear as time evolves. A number of other extensions are possible, but we seek to determine the properties of this simple model, in order to understand which extensions are necessary to capture the complexity of the web.

Examples

Undirected network models

Protein interaction networks

Vazquez proposed a growing graph based on duplication modeling protein interactions. At every time step a prototype is chosen randomly. With probability q edges of the prototype are copied. With probability p an edge to the prototype is created.[2]

Proteome networks

Sole proposed a growing graph initialized with a 5-ring substrate. At every time step a new node is added and a prototype is chosen at random. The prototype's edges are copied with a probability δ. Furthermore, random nodes are connected to the newly introduced node with probability $\alpha = \beta/N$, where δ and β are given parameters in $(0,1)$ and N is the number of total nodes at the considered time step. (see fig. 1).[3]

Directed network models

Biological networks

Middendorf-Ziv (MZ) proposed a growing directed graph modeling biological network dynamics. A prototype is chosen at random and duplicated. The prototype or progenitor node has edges pruned with probability β and edges added with probability $\alpha \ll \beta$. Based loosely on the undirected protein network model of Sole et al.[3]

WWW networks and citation networks

Vazquez proposed a growth model based on a recursive 'copying' mechanism, continuing to 2nd nearest neighbors, 3rd nearest neighbors etc. The authors call it a 'random walk' mechanism.).[4]

Growing network with copying (GNC)

Krapivsky and Redner proposed a new growing network model, which grows by adding nodes one at a time. A newly introduced node randomly selects a target node and links to it, as well as to all ancestor nodes of the target node (Fig. 2). If the target node is the initial root node, no additional links are generated by the copying mechanism. If the newly introduced node were to always choose the root node as the target, a star graph would be generated. On the other hand, if the target node is always the most recent one in the network, all previous nodes are ancestors of the target and the copying mechanism would give a complete graph. Correspondingly, the total number of links in a network of N nodes can range from $N-1$ (star graph) to $N(N-1)/2$ (complete graph). Notice also that the number of outgoing links from each new node (the out-degree) can range between 1 and the current number of nodes.[5]

Notes

[1] Kogias, A. (2005), *Int. J. Web Engineering and Technology* **2** (1).

[2] A. Vazquez, A. Flammini, A. Maritan, A. Vespignani, Modeling of protein interaction networks, arXiv:cond-mat/0108043.

[3] R. V. Sole, R. Pastor-Satorras, E. Smith, T. B. Kepler, A model of large-scale proteome evolution, arXiv.org:cond-mat/0207311.

[4] A. Vazquez, Knowing a network by walking on it: emergence of scaling, arXiv:cond-mat/0006132.

[5] Krapivsky, P. L., and Redner, S., Network growth by copying, Phys. Rev. E 71 036118 (2005).

References

• Kleinberg, J. M., R. Kumar, P. Raghavan, S. Rajagopalan, and A. Tomkins, 1999, Proceedings of the International Conference on Combinatorics and Computing.

- Kumar, R., P. Raghavan, S. Rajagopalan, D. Sivakumar, A. S. Tomkins and E. Upfal, 2000a, Proceedings of the 19th Symposium on Principles of Database Systems.
- Kumar, R., P. Raghavan, S. Rajagopalan, D. Sivakumar, A. S. Tomkins and E. Upfal, 2000b, Proceedings of the 41st IEEE Symposium on Foundations of Computer Science.

Scale-free_network

A **scale-free network** is a network whose degree distribution follows a power law, at least asymptotically. That is, the fraction $P(k)$ of nodes in the network having k connections to other nodes goes for large values of k as

where is a normalization constant and is a parameter whose value is typically in the range $2 < < 3$, although occasionally it may lie outside these bounds.

Many networks are conjectured to be scale-free, including World Wide Web links, biological networks, and social networks, although the scientific community is still discussing these claims as more sophisticated data analysis techniques become available.[1] Preferential attachment and the fitness model have been proposed as mechanisms to explain conjectured power law degree distributions in real networks.

History

In studies of the networks of citations between scientific papers, Derek de Solla Price showed in 1965 that the number of links to papers—i.e., the number of citations they receive—had a heavy-tailed distribution following a Pareto distribution or power law, and thus that the citation network is scale-free. He did not however use the term "scale-free network", which was not coined until some decades later. In a later paper in 1976, Price also proposed a mechanism to explain the occurrence of power laws in citation networks, which he called "cumulative advantage" but which is today more commonly known under the name preferential attachment.

Recent interest in scale-free networks started in 1999 with work by Albert-László Barabási and colleagues at the University of Notre Dame who mapped the topology of a portion of the World Wide Web,[2] finding that some nodes, which they called "hubs", had many more connections than others and that the network as a whole had a power-law distribution of the number of links connecting to a node. After finding that a few other networks, including some social and biological networks, also had heavy-tailed degree distributions, Barabási and collaborators coined the term "scale-free network" to describe the class of networks that exhibit a power-law degree distribution. Amaral et al. showed that most of the real-world networks can be classified into two large categories according to the decay of degree distribution P(k) for large k.

Barabási and Albert proposed a generative mechanism to explain the appearance of power-law distributions, which they called "preferential attachment" and which is essentially the same as that proposed by Price. Analytic solutions for this mechanism (also similar to the solution of Price) were presented in 2000 by Dorogovtsev, Mendes and Samukhin [3] and independently by Krapivsky, Redner, and Leyvraz, and later rigorously proved by mathematician Béla Bollobás.[4] Notably, however, this mechanism only produces a specific subset of networks in the scale-free class, and many alternative mechanisms have been discovered since.[5]

The history of scale-free networks also includes some disagreement. On an empirical level, the scale-free nature of several networks has been called into question. For instance, the three brothers Faloutsos believed that the Internet had a power law degree distribution on the basis of traceroute data; however, it has been suggested that this is a layer 3 illusion created by routers, which appear as high-degree nodes while concealing the internal layer 2 structure of the ASes they interconnect. [6] On a theoretical level, refinements to the abstract definition of scale-free have been proposed. For example, Li et al. (2005) recently offered a potentially more precise "scale-free metric". Briefly, let G be a graph with edge set E, and denote the degree of a vertex (that is, the number of edges incident to) by . Define

This is maximized when high-degree nodes are connected to other high-degree nodes. Now define

where s_{max} is the maximum value of $s(H)$ for H in the set of all graphs with degree distribution identical to G. This gives a metric between 0 and 1, where a graph G with small $S(G)$ is "scale-rich", and a graph G with $S(G)$ close to 1 is "scale-free". This definition captures the notion of self-similarity implied in the name "scale-free".

Characteristics

The most notable characteristic in a scale-free network is the relative commonness of vertices with a degree that greatly exceeds the average. The highest-degree nodes are often called "hubs", and are thought to serve specific purposes in their networks, although this depends greatly on the domain.

The scale-free property strongly correlates with the network's robustness to failure. It turns out that

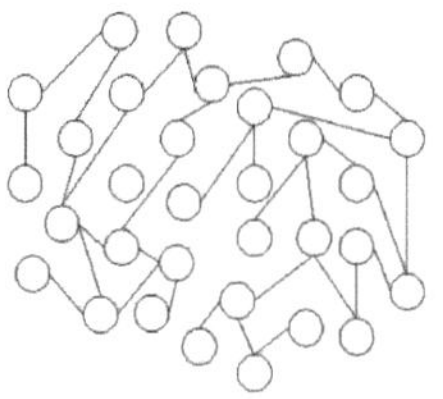 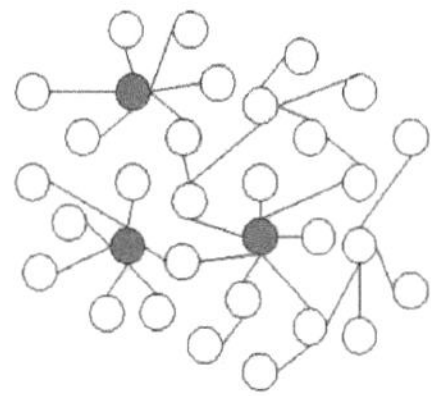

(a) Random network   (b) Scale-free network

Random network (a) and scale-free network (b). In the scale-free network, the larger hubs are highlighted.

the major hubs are closely followed by smaller ones. These ones, in turn, are followed by other nodes with an even smaller degree and so on. This hierarchy allows for a fault tolerant behavior. If failures occur at random and the vast majority of nodes are those with small degree, the likelihood that a hub would be affected is almost negligible. Even if a hub-failure occurs, the network will generally not lose its connectedness, due to the remaining hubs. On the other hand, if we choose a few major hubs and take them out of the network, the network is turned into a set of rather isolated graphs. Thus, hubs are both a strength and a weakness of scale-free networks. These properties have been studied analytically using percolation theory by Cohen et al.[7] [8] and by Callaway et al.[9]

Another important characteristic of scale-free networks is the clustering coefficient distribution, which decreases as the node degree increases. This distribution also follows a power law. This implies that the low-degree nodes belong to very dense sub-graphs and those sub-graphs are connected to each other through hubs. Consider a social network in which nodes are people and links are acquaintance relationships between people. It is easy to see that people tend to form communities, i.e., small groups in which everyone knows everyone (one can think of such community as a complete graph). In addition, the members of a community also have a few acquaintance relationships to people outside that community. Some people, however, are connected to a large number of communities (e.g., celebrities, politicians). Those people may be considered the hubs responsible for the small-world phenomenon.

At present, the more specific characteristics of scale-free networks vary with the generative mechanism used to create them. For instance, networks generated by preferential attachment typically place the high-degree vertices in the middle of the network, connecting them together to form a core, with progressively lower-degree nodes making up the regions between the core and the periphery. The random removal of even a large fraction of vertices impacts the overall connectedness of the network very little, suggesting that such topologies could be useful for security, while targeted attacks destroys the connectedness very quickly. Other scale-free networks, which place the high-degree vertices at the periphery, do not exhibit these properties. Similarly, the clustering coefficient of scale-free networks can vary significantly depending on other topological details.

A final characteristic concerns the average distance between two vertices in a network. As with most disordered networks, such as the small world network model, this distance is very small relative to a highly ordered network such as a lattice graph. Notably, an uncorrelated power-law graph having $2 < \gamma < 3$ will have ultrasmall diameter $d \sim \ln \ln N$ where N is the number of nodes in the network, as proved by Cohen and Havlin. The diameter of a growing scale-free network might be considered almost constant in practice.

Examples

Although many real-world networks are thought to be scale-free, the evidence often remains inconclusive, primarily due to the developing awareness of more rigorous data analysis techniques.[1] As such, the scale-free nature of many networks is still being debated by the scientific community. A few examples of networks claimed to be scale-free include:

- Social networks, including collaboration networks. An example that has been studied extensively is the collaboration of movie actors in films.
- Sexual partners in humans, which affects the dispersal of sexually transmitted diseases.
- Many kinds of computer networks, including the internet and the webgraph of the World Wide Web.
- Protein-Protein interaction networks.
- Semantic networks.[10]
- Airline networks.

Scale free topology has been also found in high temperature superconductors.[11] The qualities of a high-temperature superconductor — a compound in which electrons obey the laws of quantum physics, and flow in perfect synchrony, without friction — appear linked to the fractal arrangements of seemingly random oxygen atoms.

Generative models

These scale-free networks do not arise by chance alone. Erdős and Rényi (1960) studied a model of growth for graphs in which, at each step, two nodes are chosen uniformly at random and a link is inserted between them. The properties of these random graphs are different from the properties found in scale-free networks, and therefore a model for this growth process is needed.

The mostly widely known generative model for a subset of scale-free networks is Barabási and Albert's (1999) rich get richer generative model in which each new Web page creates links to existing Web pages with a probability distribution which is not uniform, but proportional to the current in-degree of Web pages. This model was originally discovered by Derek J. de Solla Price in 1965 under the term **cumulative advantage**, but did not reach popularity until Barabási rediscovered the results under its current name (BA Model). According to this process, a page with many in-links will attract more in-links than a regular page. This generates a power-law but the resulting graph differs from the actual Web graph in other properties such as the presence of small tightly connected communities. More general models and networks characteristics have been proposed and studied (for a review see the book by Dorogovtsev and Mendes).

A somewhat different generative model for Web links has been suggested by Pennock et al. (2002). They examined communities with interests in a specific topic such as the home pages of universities, public companies, newspapers or scientists, and discarded the major hubs of the Web. In this case, the distribution of links was no longer a power law but resembled a normal distribution. Based on these observations, the authors proposed a generative model that mixes preferential attachment with a baseline probability of gaining a link.

Another generative model is the **copy** model studied by Kumar et al. (2000), in which new nodes choose an existent node at random and copy a fraction of the links of the existent node. This also generates a power law.

Interestingly, the *growth* of the networks (adding new nodes) is not a necessary condition for creating a scale-free network. Dangalchev (2004) gives examples of generating static scale-free networks. Another possibility (Caldarelli et al. 2002) is to consider the structure as static and draw a link between vertices according to a particular property of the two vertices involved. Once specified the statistical distribution for these vertices properties (fitnesses), it turns out that in some circumstances also static networks develop scale-free properties.

Scale-free ideal network

In the context of network theory a **scale-free ideal network** is a random network with a degree distribution following the scale-free ideal gas density distribution. These networks have the special property of reproducing the city-size distribution and electoral results unravelling the size distribution of social groups with information theory on complex networks,[12] when a competitive cluster growth process[13] is applied to the network. In models of scale-free ideal networks it is possible to demonstrate that Dunbar's number is the cause of the phenomenon known as the 'six degrees of separation' .

See also

- Social-circles network model - a more generalized generative model for many "real-world networks" of which the scale-free network is a special case
- Random graph
- Erdős–Rényi model
- Bose-Einstein condensation: a network theory approach
- Scale invariance
- Complex network
- Webgraph

References

[1] Clauset, Aaron; Cosma Rohilla Shalizi, M. E. J Newman (2007-06-07). "Power-law distributions in empirical data". *0706.1062*. arXiv:0706.1062. doi:10.1137/070710111.

[2] Barabási, Albert-László; Albert, Réka. (October 15, 1999). "Emergence of scaling in random networks". *Science* **286** (5439): 509–512. arXiv:cond-mat/9910332. doi:10.1126/science.286.5439.509. MR2091634.

[3] Error: Bad DOI specified!

[4] Error: Bad DOI specified!

[5] Error: Bad DOI specified!

[6] Willinger, Walter; David Alderson, and John C. Doyle (2009-5). "Mathematics and the Internet: A Source of Enormous Confusion and Great Potential" (http://authors.library.caltech.edu/15631/1/Willinger2009p5466Notices_Amer._Math._Soc.pdf). *Notices of the AMS* (American Mathematical Society) **56** (5): 586–599. . Retrieved 2011-02-03.

[7] Cohen, Reoven; K. Erez, D. ben-Avraham and S. Havlin (2000). "Resilience of the Internet to Random Breakdowns" (http://link.aps.org/doi/10.1103/PhysRevLett.85.4626). *Phys. Rev. Lett.* **85**: 4626–8. Bibcode 2000PhRvL..85.4626C. doi:10.1103/PhysRevLett.85.4626. .

[8] Cohen, Reoven; K. Erez, D. ben-Avraham and S. Havlin (2001). "Breakdown of the Internet under Intentional Attack" (http://link.aps.org/doi/10.1103/PhysRevLett.86.3682). *Phys. Rev. Lett.* **86**: 3682–5. Bibcode 2001PhRvL..86.3682C. doi:10.1103/PhysRevLett.86.3682. PMID 11328053. .

[9] Callaway, Duncan S.; M. E. J. Newman, S. H. Strogatz and D. J. Watts (2000). "Network Robustness and Fragility: Percolation on Random Graphs" (http://link.aps.org/doi/10.1103/PhysRevLett.85.5468). *Phys. Rev. Lett.* **85**: 5468–71. Bibcode 2000PhRvL..85.5468C. doi:10.1103/PhysRevLett.85.5468. .

[10] Steyvers, Mark; Joshua B. Tenenbaum (2005). "The Large-Scale Structure of Semantic Networks: Statistical Analyses and a Model of Semantic Growth" (http://www.leaonline.com/doi/abs/10.1207/s15516709cog2901_3). *Cognitive Science* **29** (1): 41–78. doi:10.1207/s15516709cog2901_3. .

[11] Fratini, Michela, Poccia, Nicola, Ricci, Alessandro, Campi, Gaetano, Burghammer, Manfred, Aeppli, Gabriel Bianconi, Antonio (2010). "Scale-free structural organization of oxygen interstitials in La2CuO4+y" (http://www.nature.com/nature/journal/v466/n7308/full/nature09260.html). *Nature* **466** (7308): 841–4. doi:10.1038/nature09260. PMID 20703301. .

[12] A. Hernando, D. Villuendas, C. Vesperinas, M. Abad, A. Plastino (2009). "Unravelling the size distribution of social groups with information theory on complex networks". arXiv:0905.3704 [physics.soc-ph]., submitted to *European Physics Journal B*

[13] André A. Moreira, Demétrius R. Paula, Raimundo N. Costa Filho, José S. Andrade, Jr. (2006). "Competitive cluster growth in complex networks". arXiv:cond-mat/0603272 [cond-mat.dis-nn].

- Albert R., Barabási A.-L. (2002). "Statistical mechanics of complex networks" (http://www.nd.edu/~networks/Publication Categories/publications.htm#anchor-allpub0001). *Rev. Mod. Phys.* **74**: 47–97. Bibcode 2002RvMP...74...47A. doi:10.1103/RevModPhys.74.47.

- Amaral, LAN, Scala, A., Barthelemy, M., Stanley, HE. (2000). "Classes of behavior of small-world networks". *Proc. Natl. Acad. Sci. U.S.A.* **97** (21): 11149–52. arXiv:cond-mat/0001458. doi:10.1073/pnas.200327197. PMC 17168. PMID 11005838.
- Barabási, Albert-László (2004). *Linked: How Everything is Connected to Everything Else*. ISBN 0-452-28439-2.
- Barabási, Albert-László; Bonabeau, Eric (May 2003). "Scale-Free Networks" (http://www.nd.edu/~networks/ Publication Categories/01 Review Articles/ScaleFree_Scientific Ameri 288, 60-69 (2003).pdf) (PDF). *Scientific American* **288** (5): 60–9. doi:10.1038/scientificamerican0503-60.
- Dan Braha, Yaneer Bar-Yam (2004). "Topology of Large-Scale Engineering Problem-Solving Networks" (http:// necsi.edu/affiliates/braha/Topology--of--Large--Scale--Design--PRE69.pdf) (PDF). *Phys. Rev. E* **69**: 016113. doi:10.1103/PhysRevE.69.016113.
- Caldarelli G. " Scale-Free Networks" (http://www.oup.com/us/catalog/general/subject/Physics/ Mathematicalphysics/~~/dmlldz11c2EmY2k9OTc4MDE5OTIxMTUxNw==) Oxford University Press, Oxford (2007).
- Caldarelli G., Capocci A., De Los Rios P., Muñoz M.A. (2002). "Scale-free networks from varying vertex intrinsic fitness". *Physical Review Letters* **89** (25): 258702. arXiv:cond-mat/0207366. Bibcode 2002PhRvL..89y8702C. doi:10.1103/PhysRevLett.89.258702. PMID 12484927.
- R. Cohen, K. Erez, D. ben-Avraham and S. Havlin (2000). "Resilience of the Internet to Random Breakdowns" (http://link.aps.org/doi/10.1103/PhysRevLett.85.4626). *Phys. Rev. Lett.* **85**: 4626–8. Bibcode 2000PhRvL..85.4626C. doi:10.1103/PhysRevLett.85.4626.
- R. Cohen, K. Erez, D. ben-Avraham and S. Havlin (2001). "Breakdown of the Internet under Intentional Attack" (http://link.aps.org/doi/10.1103/PhysRevLett.86.3682). *Phys. Rev. Lett.* **86**: 3682–5. Bibcode 2001PhRvL..86.3682C. doi:10.1103/PhysRevLett.86.3682. PMID 11328053.
- A.F. Rozenfeld, R. Cohen, D. ben-Avraham, S. Havlin (2002). "Scale-free networks on lattices" (http://havlin. biu.ac.il/Publications.php?keyword=Scale-free+networks+on+lattices&year=*&match=all). *Phys. Rev. Lett.* **89**.
- Dangalchev, Ch. (2004). "Generation models for scale-free networks". *Physica A* **338**.
- Dorogovtsev, Mendes, J.F.F. , Samukhin, A.N. (2000). "Structure of Growing Networks: Exact Solution of the Barabási—Albert's Model". *Phys. Rev. Lett.* **85** (21): 4633–6. Bibcode 2000PhRvL..85.4633D. doi:10.1103/PhysRevLett.85.4633. PMID 11082614.
- Dorogovtsev, S.N., Mendes, J.F.F. (2003). *Evolution of Networks: from biological networks to the Internet and WWW*. Oxford University Press. ISBN 0-19-851590-1.
- Dorogovtsev, S.N., Goltsev A. V., Mendes, J.F.F. (2008). "Critical phenomena in complex networks". *Rev. Mod. Phys.* **80**: 1275. Bibcode 2008RvMP...80.1275D. doi:10.1103/RevModPhys.80.1275.
- Dorogovtsev, S.N., Mendes, J.F.F. (2002). "Evolution of networks". *Advances in Physics* **51**: 1079–1187. doi:10.1080/00018730110112519.
- Erdős, P.; Rényi, A. (1960) (PDF). *On the Evolution of Random Graphs* (http://www.math-inst.hu/~p_erdos/ 1960-10.pdf). **5**. Publication of the Mathematical Institute of the Hungarian Academy of Science. pp. 17–61.
- Faloutsos, M., Faloutsos, P., Faloutsos, C. (1999). "On power-law relationships of the internet topology". *Comp. Comm. Rev.* **29**: 251. doi:10.1145/316194.316229.
- Li, L., Alderson, D., Tanaka, R., Doyle, J.C., Willinger, W. (2005). "Towards a Theory of Scale-Free Graphs: Definition, Properties, and Implications (Extended Version)". arXiv:cond-mat/0501169 [cond-mat.dis-nn].
- Kumar, R., Raghavan, P., Rajagopalan, S., Sivakumar, D., Tomkins, A., Upfal, E. (2000). "Stochastic models for the web graph" (http://www.cs.brown.edu/research/webagent/focs-2000.pdf). *Proceedings of the 41st Annual Symposium on Foundations of Computer Science (FOCS)*. Redondo Beach, CA: IEEE CS Press. pp. 57–65.
- Manev R., Manev H. (2005). "The meaning of mammalian adult neurogenesis and the function of newly added neurons: the "small-world" network" (http://linkinghub.elsevier.com/retrieve/pii/S0306987704003524). *Med.*

Hypotheses **64** (1): 114–7. doi:10.1016/j.mehy.2004.05.013. PMID 15533625.

- Matlis, Jan (November 4, 2002). "Scale-Free Networks" (http://www.computerworld.com/networkingtopics/networking/story/0,10801,75539,00.html).
- Newman, Mark E.J. (2003). "The structure and function of complex networks". arXiv:cond-mat/0303516 [cond-mat.stat-mech].
- Pastor-Satorras, R., Vespignani, A. (2004). *Evolution and Structure of the Internet: A Statistical Physics Approach*. Cambridge University Press. ISBN 0-521-82698-5.
- Pennock, D.M., Flake, G.W., Lawrence, S., Glover, E.J., Giles, C.L. (2002). "Winners don't take all: Characterizing the competition for links on the web" (http://www.modelingtheweb.com/). *Proc. Natl. Acad. Sci. U.S.A.* **99** (8): 5207–11. doi:10.1073/pnas.032085699. PMC 122747. PMID 16578867.
- Robb, John. Scale-Free Networks and Terrorism (http://globalguerrillas.typepad.com/globalguerrillas/2004/05/scalefree_terro.html), 2004.
- Keller, E.F. (2005). "Revisiting "scale-free" networks" (http://www3.interscience.wiley.com/cgi-bin/abstract/112092785/ABSTRACT). *BioEssays* **27** (10): 1060–8. doi:10.1002/bies.20294. PMID 16163729.
- Onody, R.N., de Castro, P.A. (2004). "Complex Network Study of Brazilian Soccer Player". *Phys. Rev. E* **70**: 037103. arXiv:cond-mat/0409609. doi:10.1103/PhysRevE.70.037103.
- Reuven Cohen, Shlomo Havlin (2003). "Scale-Free Networks are Ultrasmall" (http://havlin.biu.ac.il/Publications.php?keyword=Scale-Free+Networks+are+Ultrasmall&year=*&match=all). *Phys. Rev. Lett.* **90** (5): 058701. arXiv:cond-mat/0205476. Bibcode 2003PhRvL..90e8701C. doi:10.1103/PhysRevLett.90.058701. PMID 12633404.

External links

- snGraph (http://digital.csic.es/handle/10261/27556) Optimal software to manage scale-free networks.
- The Erdős Webgraph Server (http://web-graph.org) describing the hyperlink structure of a weekly updated, constantly increasing portion of the WWW.

World_Wide_Web

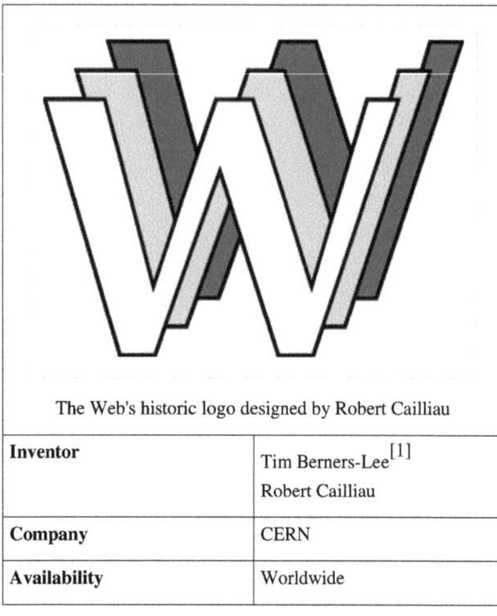

The Web's historic logo designed by Robert Cailliau

Inventor	Tim Berners-Lee[1] Robert Cailliau
Company	CERN
Availability	Worldwide

The **World Wide Web** (abbreviated as **WWW** or **W3**,[2] commonly known as **the Web**, and nickname: "information superhighway") is a system of interlinked hypertext documents accessed via the Internet. With a web browser, one can view web pages that may contain text, images, videos, and other multimedia, and navigate between them via hyperlinks.

Using concepts from his earlier hypertext systems like ENQUIRE, British engineer and computer scientist Sir Tim Berners-Lee, now Director of the World Wide Web Consortium (W3C), wrote a proposal in March 1989 for what would eventually become the World Wide Web.[1] At CERN, a European research organization near Geneva situated on Swiss and French soil,[3] Berners-Lee and Belgian computer scientist Robert Cailliau proposed in 1990 to use hypertext "... to link and access information of various kinds as a web of nodes in which the user can browse at will",[4] and they publicly introduced the project in December.[5]

History

In the May 1970 issue of *Popular Science* magazine Arthur C. Clarke was reported to have predicted that satellites would one day "bring the accumulated knowledge of the world to your fingertips" using a console that would combine the functionality of the Xerox, telephone, television and a small computer, allowing data transfer and video conferencing around the globe.[6] Clarke also determined that geosyncronous orbit would be possible at the altitude of 22,000 miles, which is why that region is called the Clarke Belt.--David Starkey (talk) 12:51, 5 May 2012 (UTC)

The NeXT Computer used by Berners-Lee. The handwritten label declares, "This machine is a server. DO NOT POWER IT DOWN!!"

In March 1989, Tim Berners-Lee wrote a proposal that referenced ENQUIRE, a database and software project he had built in 1980, and described a more elaborate information management system.[7]

With help from Robert Cailliau, he published a more formal proposal (on November 12, 1990) to build a "Hypertext project" called "WorldWideWeb" (one word, also "W3") as a "web" of "hypertext documents" to be viewed by "browsers" using a client–server architecture.[4] This proposal estimated that a read-only web would be developed within three months and that it would take six months to achieve "the creation of new links and new material by readers, [so that] authorship becomes universal" as well as "the automatic notification of a reader when new material of interest to him/her has become available." While the read-only goal was met, accessible authorship of web content took longer to mature, with the wiki concept, blogs, Web 2.0 and RSS/Atom.[8]

The proposal was modeled after the Dynatext SGML reader by Electronic Book Technology, a spin-off from the Institute for Research in Information and Scholarship at Brown University. The Dynatext system, licensed by CERN, was technically advanced and was a key player in the extension of SGML ISO 8879:1986 to Hypermedia within HyTime, but it was considered too expensive and had an inappropriate licensing policy for use in the general high energy physics community, namely a fee for each document and each document alteration.

The CERN datacenter in 2010 housing some WWW servers

A NeXT Computer was used by Berners-Lee as the world's first web server and also to write the first web browser, WorldWideWeb, in 1990. By Christmas 1990, Berners-Lee had built all the tools necessary for a working Web:[9] the first web browser (which was a web editor as well); the first web server; and the first web pages,[10] which described the project itself. On August 6, 1991, he posted a short summary of the World Wide Web project on the `alt.hypertext` newsgroup.[11] This date also marked the debut of the Web as a publicly available service on the Internet. The first photo on the web was uploaded by Berners-Lee in 1992, an image of the CERN house band Les Horribles Cernettes.

Web as a "Side Effect" of the 40 years of Particle Physics Experiments.

It happened many times during history of science that the most impressive results of large scale scientific efforts appeared far away from the main directions of those efforts [...] After the World War 2 the nuclear centers of almost all developed countries became the places with the highest concentration of talented scientists. For about four decades many of them were invited to the international CERN's Laboratories. So specific kind of the CERN's intellectual "entire culture" (as you called it) was constantly growing from one generation of the scientists and engineers to another. When the concentration of the human talents per square foot of the CERN's Labs reached the critical mass, it caused an intellectual explosion

The Web, – crucial point of human's history, was born... Nothing could be compared to it [...] We cant imagine yet the real scale of the recent shake, because there has not been so fast growing multi-dimension social-economic processes in human history...[12]

The first server outside Europe was set up at SLAC to host the SPIRES-HEP database. Accounts differ substantially as to the date of this event. The World Wide Web Consortium says December 1992,[13] whereas SLAC itself claims 1991.[14] [15] This is supported by a W3C document entitled *A Little History of the World Wide Web*.[16]

The crucial underlying concept of hypertext originated with older projects from the 1960s, such as the Hypertext Editing System (HES) at Brown University, Ted Nelson's Project Xanadu, and Douglas Engelbart's oN-Line System (NLS). Both Nelson and Engelbart were in turn inspired by Vannevar Bush's microfilm-based "memex", which was described in the 1945 essay "As We May Think".

[17]

Berners-Lee's breakthrough was to marry hypertext to the Internet. In his book *Weaving The Web*, he explains that he had repeatedly suggested that a marriage between the two technologies was possible to members of *both* technical communities, but when no one took up his invitation, he finally tackled the project himself. In the process, he developed three essential technologies:

1. a system of globally unique identifiers for resources on the Web and elsewhere, the Universal Document Identifier (UDI), later known as Uniform Resource Locator (URL) and Uniform Resource Identifier (URI);
2. the publishing language HyperText Markup Language (HTML);
3. the Hypertext Transfer Protocol (HTTP).[18]

The World Wide Web had a number of differences from other hypertext systems that were then available. The Web required only unidirectional links rather than bidirectional ones. This made it possible for someone to link to another resource without action by the owner of that resource. It also significantly reduced the difficulty of implementing web servers and browsers (in comparison to earlier systems), but in turn presented the chronic problem of *link rot*. Unlike predecessors such as HyperCard, the World Wide Web was non-proprietary, making it possible to develop servers and clients independently and to add extensions without licensing restrictions. On April 30, 1993, CERN announced that the World Wide Web would be free to anyone, with no fees due.[19] Coming two months after the announcement that the server implementation of the Gopher protocol was no longer free to use, this produced a rapid shift away from Gopher and towards the Web. An early popular web browser was ViolaWWW for Unix and the X Windowing System.

Scholars generally agree that a turning point for the World Wide Web began with the introduction[20] of the Mosaic web browser[21] in 1993, a graphical browser developed by a team at the National Center for Supercomputing Applications at the University of Illinois at Urbana-Champaign (NCSA-UIUC), led by Marc Andreessen. Funding for Mosaic came from the U.S. *High-Performance Computing and Communications Initiative* and the *High Performance Computing and Communication Act of 1991*, one of several computing developments initiated by U.S. Senator Al Gore.[22] Prior to the release of Mosaic, graphics were not commonly mixed with text in web pages and the Web's popularity was less than older protocols in use over the Internet, such as Gopher and Wide Area Information Servers (WAIS). Mosaic's

Robert Cailliau, Jean-François Abramatic and Tim Berners-Lee at the 10th anniversary of the World Wide Web Consortium.

graphical user interface allowed the Web to become, by far, the most popular Internet protocol.

The World Wide Web Consortium (W3C) was founded by Tim Berners-Lee after he left the European Organization for Nuclear Research (CERN) in October 1994. It was founded at the Massachusetts Institute of Technology Laboratory for Computer Science (MIT/LCS) with support from the Defense Advanced Research Projects Agency (DARPA), which had pioneered the Internet; a year later, a second site was founded at INRIA (a French national computer research lab) with support from the European Commission DG InfSo; and in 1996, a third continental site was created in Japan at Keio University. By the end of 1994, while the total number of websites was still minute compared to present standards, quite a number of notable websites were already active, many of which are the precursors or inspiration for today's most popular services.

Connected by the existing Internet, other websites were created around the world, adding international standards for domain names and HTML. Since then, Berners-Lee has played an active role in guiding the development of web standards (such as the markup languages in which web pages are composed), and in recent years has advocated his vision of a Semantic Web. The World Wide Web enabled the spread of information over the Internet through an easy-to-use and flexible format. It thus played an important role in popularizing use of the Internet.[23] Although the two terms are sometimes conflated in popular use, *World Wide Web* is not synonymous with *Internet*.[24] The Web is a collection of documents and both client and server software using Internet protocols such as TCP/IP and HTTP.

Function

The terms Internet and World Wide Web are often used in everyday speech without much distinction. However, the Internet and the World Wide Web are not one and the same. The Internet is a global system of interconnected computer networks. In contrast, the Web is one of the services that runs on the Internet. It is a collection of text documents and other resources, linked by hyperlinks and URLs, usually accessed by web browsers from web servers. In short, the Web can be thought of as an application "running" on the Internet.[25]

Viewing a web page on the World Wide Web normally begins either by typing the URL of the page into a web browser or by following a hyperlink to that page or resource. The web browser then initiates a series of communication messages, behind the scenes, in order to fetch and display it. As an example, consider accessing a page with the URL `http://example.org/wiki/World_Wide_Web` .

First, the browser resolves the server-name portion of the URL (*example.org*) into an Internet Protocol address using the globally distributed database known as the Domain Name System (DNS); this lookup returns an IP address such as *208.80.152.2*. The browser then requests the resource by sending an HTTP request across the Internet to the computer at that particular address. It makes the request to a particular application port in the underlying Internet Protocol Suite so that the computer receiving the request can distinguish an HTTP request from other network protocols it may be servicing such as e-mail delivery; the HTTP protocol normally uses port 80. The content of the HTTP request can be as simple as the two lines of text

```
GET /wiki/World_Wide_Web HTTP/1.1
Host: example.org
```

The computer receiving the HTTP request delivers it to web server software listening for requests on port 80. If the web server can fulfill the request it sends an HTTP response back to the browser indicating success, which can be as simple as

```
HTTP/1.0 200 OK
Content-Type: text/html; charset=UTF-8
```

followed by the content of the requested page. The Hypertext Markup Language for a basic web page looks like

```
<html>
<head>
<title>Example.org — The World Wide Web</title>
</head>
<body>
<p>The World Wide Web, abbreviated as WWW and commonly known ...</p>
</body>
</html>
```

The web browser parses the HTML, interpreting the markup (`<title>`, `<p>` for paragraph, and such) that surrounds the words in order to draw the text on the screen.

Many web pages use HTML to reference the URLs of other resources such as images, other embedded media, scripts that affect page behavior, and Cascading Style Sheets that affect page layout. The browser will make additional HTTP requests to the web server for these other Internet media types. As it receives their content from the web server, the browser progressively renders the page onto the screen as specified by its HTML and these additional resources.

Linking

Most web pages contain hyperlinks to other related pages and perhaps to downloadable files, source documents, definitions and other web resources. In the underlying HTML, a hyperlink looks like

```
<a href="http://example.org/wiki/Main_Page">Example.org, a free encyclopedia</a>
```

Such a collection of useful, related resources, interconnected via hypertext links is dubbed a *web* of information. Publication on the Internet created what Tim Berners-Lee first called the *WorldWideWeb* (in its original CamelCase, which was subsequently discarded) in November 1990.[4]

The hyperlink structure of the WWW is described by the webgraph: the nodes of the webgraph correspond to the web pages (or URLs) the directed edges between them to the hyperlinks.

Over time, many web resources pointed to by hyperlinks disappear, relocate, or are replaced with different content. This makes hyperlinks obsolete, a phenomenon referred to in some circles as link rot and the

Graphic representation of a minute fraction of the WWW, demonstrating hyperlinks

hyperlinks affected by it are often called dead links. The ephemeral nature of the Web has prompted many efforts to archive web sites. The Internet Archive, active since 1996, is one of the best-known efforts.

Dynamic updates of web pages

JavaScript is a scripting language that was initially developed in 1995 by Brendan Eich, then of Netscape, for use within web pages.[26] The standardized version is ECMAScript.[26] To overcome some of the limitations of the page-by-page model described above, some web applications also use Ajax (asynchronous JavaScript and XML). JavaScript is delivered with the page that can make additional HTTP requests to the server, either in response to user actions such as mouse-clicks or based on lapsed time. The server's responses are used to modify the current page rather than creating a new page with each response. Thus, the server must provide only limited, incremental information. Since multiple Ajax requests can be handled at the same time, users can interact with a page even while data is being retrieved. Some web applications regularly poll the server to ask whether new information is available.[27]

WWW prefix

Many domain names used for the World Wide Web begin with *www* because of the long-standing practice of naming Internet hosts (servers) according to the services they provide. The hostname for a web server is often *www*, in the same way that it may be *ftp* for an FTP server, and *news* or *nntp* for a USENET news server. These host names appear as Domain Name System or [domain name server](DNS) subdomain names, as in `www.example.com`. The use of 'www' as a subdomain name is not required by any technical or policy standard; indeed, the first ever web server was called `nxoc01.cern.ch`,[28] and many web sites exist without it. According to Paolo Palazzi,[29] who worked at CERN along with Tim Berners-Lee, the popular use of 'www' subdomain was accidental; the World Wide Web project page was intended to be published at www.cern.ch while info.cern.ch was intended to be the CERN home page, however the dns records were never switched, and the practice of prepending 'www' to an institution's website domain name was subsequently copied. Many established websites still use 'www', or they invent other subdomain names such as 'www2', 'secure', etc. Many such web servers are set up such that both the domain root (e.g., example.com) and the *www* subdomain (e.g., www.example.com) refer to the same site; others require one form or the other, or they may map to different web sites.

The use of a subdomain name is useful for load balancing incoming web traffic by creating a CNAME record that points to a cluster of web servers. Since, currently, only a subdomain can be used in a CNAME, the same result cannot be achieved by using the bare domain root.

When a user submits an incomplete domain name to a web browser in its address bar input field, some web browsers automatically try adding the prefix "www" to the beginning of it and possibly ".com", ".org" and ".net" at the end, depending on what might be missing. For example, entering 'microsoft' may be transformed to *http://www.microsoft.com/* and 'openoffice' to *http://www.openoffice.org*. This feature started appearing in early versions of Mozilla Firefox, when it still had the working title 'Firebird' in early 2003, from an earlier practice in browsers such as Lynx.[30] It is reported that Microsoft was granted a US patent for the same idea in 2008, but only for mobile devices.[31]

In English, *www* is pronounced by individually pronouncing the name of characters (*double-u double-u double-u*) or by saying the phrase "triple double-u". Although some technical users pronounce it *dub-dub-dub*, this is not widespread (although is commonly used by the general public in New Zealand). The English writer Douglas Adams once quipped in The Independent on Sunday (1999): "The World Wide Web is the only thing I know of whose shortened form takes three times longer to say than what it's short for," with Stephen Fry later pronouncing it in his "Podgrammes" series of podcasts as "wuh wuh wuh." In Mandarin Chinese, *World Wide Web* is commonly translated via a phono-semantic matching to *wàn wéi wǎng* (), which satisfies *www* and literally means "myriad dimensional net",[32] a translation that very appropriately reflects the design concept and proliferation of the World Wide Web. Tim Berners-Lee's web-space states that *World Wide Web* is officially spelled as three separate words, each capitalized, with no intervening hyphens.[33]

Use of the www prefix is declining as Web 2.0 web applications seek to brand their domain names and make them easily pronounceable.[34] As the mobile web grows in popularity, services like Gmail.com, MySpace.com, Facebook.com and Twitter.com are most often discussed without adding the www to the domain (or the .com).

Specifiers: http and https

The scheme specifiers (*http://* or *https://*) in URIs refer to the Hypertext Transfer Protocol and to HTTP Secure, respectively, and so define the communication protocol to be used for the request and response. The HTTP protocol is fundamental to the operation of the World Wide Web; the added encryption layer in HTTPS is essential when confidential information such as passwords or banking information are to be exchanged over the public Internet. Web browsers usually prepend the scheme to URLs too, if omitted.

Web Servers

The primary function of a web server is to deliver web pages on the request to clients. This means delivery of HTML documents and any additional content that may be included by a document, such as images, style sheets and scripts.

Privacy

It is possible that average computer users who use the World Wide Web mainly for things like entertainment may have surrendered their right to privacy in exchange for using a number of services available on the World Wide Web.[35] For example: more than half a billion people worldwide have used a social network service,[36] and of the generations of people within the United States who have had access to the internet from a young age, half have some form of Social Networking presence.[37] and are part of a generational shift that could be changing norms.[38] [39] The social network Facebook progressed from U.S. college students to a 70% non-U.S. audience, but in 2009 estimated that only 20% of its members use privacy settings.[40] In 2010 (six years after co-founding the company), Mark Zuckerberg wrote, "we will add privacy controls that are much simpler to use".[41]

Privacy representatives from 60 countries have resolved to ask for laws to complement industry self-regulation, for education for children and other minors who use the Web, and for default protections for users of social networks.[42] They also believe data protection for personally identifiable information benefits business more than the sale of that information.[42] Users can opt-in to features in browsers to clear their personal histories locally and block some cookies and advertising networks[43] but they are still tracked in websites' server logs, and in particular web beacons.[44] Berners-Lee and colleagues see hope in accountability and appropriate use achieved by extending the Web's architecture to policy awareness, perhaps with audit logging, reasoners and appliances.[45]

In exchange for providing free content, vendors hire advertisers who spy on Web users and base their business model on tracking them.[46] Since 2009, they buy and sell consumer data on exchanges (lacking a few details that could make it possible to de-anonymize, or identify an individual).[46] [47] Hundreds of millions of times per day, Lotame Solutions captures what users are typing in real time, and sends that text to OpenAmplify who then tries to determine, to quote a writer at *The Wall Street Journal*, "what topics are being discussed, how the author feels about those topics, and what the person is going to do about them".[48] [49]

Microsoft backed away in 2008 from its plans for strong privacy features in Internet Explorer,[50] leaving its users (50% of the world's Web users) open to advertisers who may make assumptions about them based on only one click when they visit a website.[51] Among services paid for by advertising, Yahoo! could collect the most data about users of commercial websites, about 2,500 bits of information per month about each typical user of its site and its affiliated advertising network sites. Yahoo! was followed by MySpace with about half that potential and then by AOL–TimeWarner, Google, Facebook, Microsoft, and eBay.[52]

Security

The Web has become criminals' preferred pathway for spreading malware. Cybercrime carried out on the Web can include identity theft, fraud, espionage and intelligence gathering.[] Web-based vulnerabilities now outnumber traditional computer security concerns,[53] [54] and as measured by Google, about one in ten web pages may contain malicious code.[55] Most Web-based attacks take place on legitimate websites, and most, as measured by Sophos, are hosted in the United States, China and Russia.[56] The most common of all malware threats is SQL injection attacks against websites.[57] Through HTML and URIs the Web was vulnerable to attacks like cross-site scripting (XSS) that came with the introduction of JavaScript[58] and were exacerbated to some degree by Web 2.0 and Ajax web design that favors the use of scripts.[59] Today by one estimate, 70% of all websites are open to XSS attacks on their users.[60]

Proposed solutions vary to extremes. Large security vendors like McAfee already design governance and compliance suites to meet post-9/11 regulations,[61] and some, like Finjan have recommended active real-time inspection of code and all content regardless of its source.[62] Some have argued that for enterprise to see security as a business opportunity rather than a cost center,[63] "ubiquitous, always-on digital rights management" enforced in the infrastructure by a handful of organizations must replace the hundreds of companies that today secure data and networks.[64] Jonathan Zittrain has said users sharing responsibility for computing safety is far preferable to locking down the Internet.[65]

Standards

Many formal standards and other technical specifications and software define the operation of different aspects of the World Wide Web, the Internet, and computer information exchange. Many of the documents are the work of the World Wide Web Consortium (W3C), headed by Berners-Lee, but some are produced by the Internet Engineering Task Force (IETF) and other organizations.

Usually, when web standards are discussed, the following publications are seen as foundational:

- Recommendations for markup languages, especially HTML and XHTML, from the W3C. These define the structure and interpretation of hypertext documents.
- Recommendations for stylesheets, especially CSS, from the W3C.
- Standards for ECMAScript (usually in the form of JavaScript), from Ecma International.
- Recommendations for the Document Object Model, from W3C.

Additional publications provide definitions of other essential technologies for the World Wide Web, including, but not limited to, the following:

- *Uniform Resource Identifier* (URI), which is a universal system for referencing resources on the Internet, such as hypertext documents and images. URIs, often called URLs, are defined by the IETF's RFC 3986 / STD 66: *Uniform Resource Identifier (URI): Generic Syntax*, as well as its predecessors and numerous URI scheme-defining RFCs;
- *HyperText Transfer Protocol (HTTP)*, especially as defined by RFC 2616: *HTTP/1.1* and RFC 2617: *HTTP Authentication*, which specify how the browser and server authenticate each other.

Accessibility

Access to the Web is for everyone regardless of disability—including visual, auditory, physical, speech, cognitive, and neurological. Accessibility features also help others with temporary disabilities like a broken arm or the aging population as their abilities change.[66] The Web is used for receiving information as well as providing information and interacting with society, making it essential that the Web be accessible in order to provide equal access and equal opportunity to people with disabilities.[67] Tim Berners-Lee once noted, "The power of the Web is in its universality. Access by everyone regardless of disability is an essential aspect."[66] Many countries regulate web accessibility as a requirement for websites.[68] International cooperation in the W3C Web Accessibility Initiative led to simple guidelines that web content authors as well as software developers can use to make the Web accessible to persons who may or may not be using assistive technology.[66] [69]

Internationalization

The W3C Internationalization Activity assures that web technology will work in all languages, scripts, and cultures.[70] Beginning in 2004 or 2005, Unicode gained ground and eventually in December 2007 surpassed both ASCII and Western European as the Web's most frequently used character encoding.[71] Originally RFC 3986 allowed resources to be identified by URI in a subset of US-ASCII. RFC 3987 allows more characters—any character in the Universal Character Set—and now a resource can be identified by IRI in any language.[72]

Statistics

Between 2005 and 2010, the number of Web users doubled, and was expected to surpass two billion in 2010.[73] Early studies in 1998 and 1999 estimating the size of the web using capture/recapture methods showed that the much of the web was not indexed by search engines and the web was much larger than expected,[74] [75] . According to a 2001 study, there were a massive number, over 550 billion, of documents on the Web, mostly in the invisible Web, or Deep Web.[76] A 2002 survey of 2,024 million Web pages[77] determined that by far the most Web content was in

English: 56.4%; next were pages in German (7.7%), French (5.6%), and Japanese (4.9%). A more recent study, which used Web searches in 75 different languages to sample the Web, determined that there were over 11.5 billion Web pages in the publicly indexable Web as of the end of January 2005.[78] As of March 2009, the indexable web contains at least 25.21 billion pages.[79] On July 25, 2008, Google software engineers Jesse Alpert and Nissan Hajaj announced that Google Search had discovered one trillion unique URLs.[80] As of May 2009, over 109.5 million domains operated.[81] Of these 74% were commercial or other sites operating in the .com generic top-level domain.[81]

Statistics measuring a website's popularity are usually based either on the number of page views or on associated server 'hits' (file requests) that it receives.

Speed issues

Frustration over congestion issues in the Internet infrastructure and the high latency that results in slow browsing has led to a pejorative name for the World Wide Web: the *World Wide Wait*.[82] Speeding up the Internet is an ongoing discussion over the use of peering and QoS technologies. Other solutions to reduce the congestion can be found at W3C.[83] Guidelines for Web response times are:[84]

- 0.1 second (one tenth of a second). Ideal response time. The user does not sense any interruption.
- 1 second. Highest acceptable response time. Download times above 1 second interrupt the user experience.
- 10 seconds. Unacceptable response time. The user experience is interrupted and the user is likely to leave the site or system.

Caching

If a user revisits a Web page after only a short interval, the page data may not need to be re-obtained from the source Web server. Almost all web browsers cache recently obtained data, usually on the local hard drive. HTTP requests sent by a browser will usually ask only for data that has changed since the last download. If the locally cached data are still current, it will be reused. Caching helps reduce the amount of Web traffic on the Internet. The decision about expiration is made independently for each downloaded file, whether image, stylesheet, JavaScript, HTML, or whatever other content the site may provide. Thus even on sites with highly dynamic content, many of the basic resources need to be refreshed only occasionally. Web site designers find it worthwhile to collate resources such as CSS data and JavaScript into a few site-wide files so that they can be cached efficiently. This helps reduce page download times and lowers demands on the Web server.

There are other components of the Internet that can cache Web content. Corporate and academic firewalls often cache Web resources requested by one user for the benefit of all. (See also Caching proxy server.) Some search engines also store cached content from websites. Apart from the facilities built into Web servers that can determine when files have been updated and so need to be re-sent, designers of dynamically generated Web pages can control the HTTP headers sent back to requesting users, so that transient or sensitive pages are not cached. Internet banking and news sites frequently use this facility. Data requested with an HTTP 'GET' is likely to be cached if other conditions are met; data obtained in response to a 'POST' is assumed to depend on the data that was POSTed and so is not cached.

See also

- Electronic publishing
- Lists of websites
- Prestel
- Streaming media
- Web 1.0
- Webgraph

References

[1] Quittner, Joshua (March 29, 1999). "Tim Berners Lee — Time 100 People of the Century" (http://www.time.com/time/magazine/article/ 0,9171,990627,00.html). Time Magazine. . Retrieved 17 May 2010. "He wove the World Wide Web and created a mass medium for the 21st century. The World Wide Web is Berners-Lee's alone. He designed it. He loosed it on the world. And he more than anyone else has fought to keep it open, nonproprietary and free. ."

[2] "World Wide Web Consortium" (http://www.w3.org/). . "The World Wide Web Consortium (W3C)..."

[3] Le Web a été inventé... en France ! - Le Point (http://www.lepoint.fr/technologie/ le-web-a-ete-invente-en-france-31-01-2012-1425943_58.php)

[4] "Berners-Lee, Tim; Cailliau, Robert (November 12, 1990). "WorldWideWeb: Proposal for a hypertexts Project" (http://w3.org/Proposal. html). . Retrieved July 27, 2009.

[5] Berners-Lee, Tim. "Pre-W3C Web and Internet Background" (http://w3.org/2004/Talks/w3c10-HowItAllStarted/?n=15). World Wide Web Consortium. . Retrieved April 21, 2009.

[6] von Braun, Wernher (May 1970). "TV Broadcast Satellite" (http://www.popsci.com/archive-viewer?id=8QAAAAAAMBAJ&pg=66& query=a+c+clarke). *Popular Science*: 65–66. . Retrieved January 12, 2011.

[7] Berners-Lee, Tim (March 1989). "Information Management: A Proposal" (http://w3.org/History/1989/proposal.html). W3C. . Retrieved July 27, 2009.

[8] "Tim Berners-Lee's original World Wide Web browser" (http://info.cern.ch/NextBrowser.html). . "With recent phenomena like blogs and wikis, the web is beginning to develop the kind of collaborative nature that its inventor envisaged from the start."

[9] "Tim Berners-Lee: client" (http://w3.org/People/Berners-Lee/WorldWideWeb). W3.org. . Retrieved July 27, 2009.

[10] "First Web pages" (http://w3.org/History/19921103-hypertext/hypertext/WWW/TheProject.html). W3.org. . Retrieved July 27, 2009.

[11] "Short summary of the World Wide Web project" (http://groups.google.com/group/alt.hypertext/msg/395f282a67a1916c). Groups.google.com. August 6, 1991. . Retrieved July 27, 2009.

[12] Roads and Crossroads of Internet History (http://www.netvalley.com/cgi-bin/intval/net_history.pl?chapter=2) by Gregory Gromov

[13] "W3C timeline" (http://w3.org/2005/01/timelines/timeline-2500x998.png). . Retrieved March 30, 2010.

[14] "About SPIRES" (http://slac.stanford.edu/spires/about/). . Retrieved March 30, 2010.

[15] "The Early World Wide Web at SLAC" (http://www.slac.stanford.edu/history/earlyweb/history.shtml). .

[16] "A Little History of the World Wide Web" (http://www.w3.org/History.html). .

[17] Conklin, Jeff (1987), *IEEE Computer* **20** (9): 17-41

[18] "Inventor of the Week Archive: The World Wide Web" (http://web.mit.edu/invent/iow/berners-lee.html). Massachusetts Institute of Technology: MIT School of Engineering. . Retrieved July 23, 2009.

[19] "Ten Years Public Domain for the Original Web Software" (http://tenyears-www.web.cern.ch/tenyears-www/Welcome.html). Tenyears-www.web.cern.ch. April 30, 2003. . Retrieved July 27, 2009.

[20] "Mosaic Web Browser History — NCSA, Marc Andreessen, Eric Bina" (http://livinginternet.com/w/wi_mosaic.htm). Livinginternet.com. . Retrieved July 27, 2009.

[21] "NCSA Mosaic — September 10, 1993 Demo" (http://totic.org/nscp/demodoc/demo.html). Totic.org. . Retrieved July 27, 2009.

[22] "Vice President Al Gore's ENIAC Anniversary Speech" (http://cs.washington.edu/homes/lazowska/faculty.lecture/innovation/gore. html). Cs.washington.edu. February 14, 1996. . Retrieved July 27, 2009.

[23] "Internet legal definition of Internet" (http://legal-dictionary.thefreedictionary.com/Internet). *West's Encyclopedia of American Law, edition 2*. Free Online Law Dictionary. July 15, 2009. . Retrieved November 25, 2008.

[24] "WWW (World Wide Web) Definition" (http://techterms.com/definition/www). TechTerms. . Retrieved february 19 2010.

[25] "The W3C Technology Stack" (http://www.w3.org/Consortium/technology). World Wide Web Consortium. . Retrieved April 21, 2009.

[26] Hamilton, Naomi (July 31, 2008). "The A-Z of Programming Languages: JavaScript" (http://computerworld.com.au/article/255293/ -z_programming_languages_javascript). *Computerworld*. IDG. . Retrieved May 12, 2009.

[27] Buntin, Seth (23 September 2008). "jQuery Polling plugin" (http://buntin.org/2008/sep/23/jquery-polling-plugin/). . Retrieved 2009-08-22.

[28] Berners-Lee, Tim. "Frequently asked questions by the Press" (http://w3.org/People/Berners-Lee/FAQ.html). W3C. . Retrieved July 27, 2009.

[29] Palazzi, P (2011) 'The Early Days of the WWW at CERN' (http://soft-shake.ch/2011/en/conference/sessions.html?key=earlydays)

[30] "automatically adding www.___.com" (http://forums.mozillazine.org/viewtopic.php?f=9&t=10980). mozillaZine. May 16, 2003. . Retrieved May 27, 2009.

[31] Masnick, Mike (July 7, 2008). "Microsoft Patents Adding 'www.' And '.com' To Text" (http://techdirt.com/articles/20080626/ 0203581527.shtml). Techdirt. . Retrieved May 27, 2009.

[32] "MDBG Chinese-English dictionary — Translate" (http://us.mdbg.net/chindict/chindict.php?page=translate&trst=0&trqs=World+ Wide+Web&trlang=&wddmtm=0). . Retrieved July 27, 2009.

[33] "Frequently asked questions by the Press — Tim BL" (http://w3.org/People/Berners-Lee/FAQ.html). W3.org. . Retrieved July 27, 2009.

[34] "It's not your grandfather's Internet" (http://findarticles.com/p/articles/mi_hb6421/is_4_92/ai_n56479358/). *Strategic Finance*. 2010. .

[35] Abelson, Hal; Ledeen, Ken; Lewis, Harry Lewis (April 14, 2008). "1–2" (http://bitsbook.com/). *Blown to Bits: Your Life, Liberty, and Happiness After the Digital Explosion*. Addison Wesley. ISBN 0-13-713559-9. . Retrieved November 6, 2008.

[36] "Social Networking Explodes Worldwide as Sites Increase their Focus on Cultural Relevance" (http://comscore.com/press/release. asp?press=2396) (Press release). comScore. August 12, 2008. . Retrieved November 9, 2008.

[37] Lenhart, Amanda; Madden, Mary (April 18, 2007). "Teens, Privacy & Online Social Networks" (http://web.archive.org/web/ 20080306031923/http://www.pewinternet.org/pdfs/PIP_Teens_Privacy_SNS_Report_Final.pdf) (PDF). Pew Internet & American Life Project. Archived from the original (http://www.pewinternet.org/pdfs/PIP_Teens_Privacy_SNS_Report_Final.pdf) on 2008-03-06. . Retrieved November 9, 2008.

[38] Schmidt, Eric (Google) (October 20, 2008). *Eric Schmidt at Bloomberg on the Future of Technology* (http://youtube.com/ watch?v=rD_x9LW5QRg). YouTube. Event occurs at 16:30. . Retrieved November 9, 2008.

[39] Nussbaum, Emily (February 12, 2007). "Say Everything" (http://nymag.com/news/features/27341/). *New York* (New York Media). . Retrieved November 9, 2008.

[40] Stone, Brad (March 28, 2009). "Is Facebook Growing Up Too Fast?" (http://nytimes.com/2009/03/29/technology/internet/29face. html?pagewanted=all). *The New York Times*. . and Lee Byron (Facebook) (March 28, 2009). "The Road to 200 Million" (http://nytimes.com/ imagepages/2009/03/29/business/29face.graf01.ready.html). *The New York Times*. . Retrieved April 2, 2009.

[41] Zuckerberg, Mark (May 24, 2010). "From Facebook, answering privacy concerns with new settings" (http://www.washingtonpost.com/ wp-dyn/content/article/2010/05/23/AR2010052303828.html). *The Washington Post*. . Retrieved May 24, 2010.

[42] "Protecting privacy in a borderless world" (http://wayback.archive.org/web/*/http://www.privacyconference2008.org/pdf/ press_final_en.pdf) (PDF) (Press release). 30th International Conference of Data Protection and Privacy Commissioners, via Internet Archive. October 17, 2008. . Retrieved November 8, 2008.

[43] Cooper, Alissa (October 2008). "Browser Privacy Features: A Work In Progress" (http://www.cdt.org/privacy/20081022_browser_priv. pdf) (PDF). Center for Democracy and Technology. . Retrieved November 8, 2008.

[44] Joshua Gomez, Travis Pinnick, and Ashkan Soltani (June 1, 2009). "KnowPrivacy" (http://www.knowprivacy.org/report/ KnowPrivacy_Final_Report.pdf) (PDF). University of California, Berkeley, School of Information. pp. 8–9. . Retrieved June 2, 2009.

[45] Daniel J. Weitzner, Harold Abelson, Tim Berners-Lee, Joan Feigenbaum, James Hendler, Gerald Jay Sussman (June 13, 2007). "Information Accountability". MIT Computer Science and Artificial Intelligence Laboratory. hdl:1721.1/37600.

[46] Angwin, Julia (July 30, 2010). "The Web's New Gold Mine: Your Secrets" (http://online.wsj.com/article/ SB10001424052748703940904575395073512989404.html). *The Wall Street Journal* (Dow Jones). . Retrieved August 3, 2010.

[47] Steel, Emily and Angwin, Julia (August 4, 2010). "On the Web's Cutting Edge, Anonymity in Name Only" (http://online.wsj.com/article/ SB10001424052748703294904575385532109190198.html). *The Wall Street Journal* (Dow Jones). . Retrieved August 3, 2010.

[48] Angwin, Julia and Valentino-DeVries, Jennifer (July 30, 2010). "Analyzing What You Have Typed" (http://blogs.wsj.com/digits/2010/ 07/30/analyzing-what-you-have-typed/). *The Wall Street Journal* (Dow Jones). . Retrieved August 3, 2010.

[49] Valentino-Devries, Jennifer (July 31, 2010). "What They Know About You" (http://online.wsj.com/article/ SB10001424052748703999304575399041849931612.html). *The Wall Street Journal* (Dow Jones). . Retrieved August 3, 2010.

[50] Wingfield, Nick (August 2, 2010). "Microsoft Quashed Effort to Boost Online Privacy" (http://web.archive.org/web/20110101183148/ http://online.wsj.com/article/SB10001424052748703467304575383530439838568.html). *The Wall Street Journal* (Dow Jones). Archived from the original (http://online.wsj.com/article/SB10001424052748703467304575383530439838568.html) on 2011-01-01. . Retrieved August 3, 2010.

[51] Steel, Emily and Angwin, Julia (August 4, 2010). "One Smart Cookie" (http://online.wsj.com/article/ SB10001424052748704017904575409021400239454.html). *The Wall Street Journal* (Dow Jones). . Retrieved August 3, 2010.

[52] Story, Louise and comScore (March 10, 2008). "They Know More Than You Think" (http://www.nytimes.com/imagepages/2008/03/ 10/technology/20080310_PRIVACY_GRAPHIC.html) (JPEG). *The New York Times*. . in Story, Louise (March 10, 2008). "To Aim Ads, Web Is Keeping Closer Eye on You" (http://www.nytimes.com/2008/03/10/technology/10privacy.html). *The New York Times* (The New York Times Company). . Retrieved March 9, 2008.

[53] Christey, Steve and Martin, Robert A. (May 22, 2007). "Vulnerability Type Distributions in CVE (version 1.1)" (http://cwe.mitre.org/ documents/vuln-trends/index.html). MITRE Corporation. . Retrieved June 7, 2008.

[54] (PDF) *Symantec Internet Security Threat Report: Trends for July–December 2007 (Executive Summary)* (http://eval.symantec.com/ mktginfo/enterprise/white_papers/b-whitepaper_exec_summary_internet_security_threat_report_xiii_04-2008.en-us.pdf). **XIII**. Symantec Corp.. April 2008. pp. 1–2. . Retrieved May 11, 2008.

[55] "Google searches web's dark side" (http://news.bbc.co.uk/2/hi/technology/6645895.stm). BBC News. May 11, 2007. . Retrieved April 26, 2008.

[56] "Security Threat Report" (http://www.sophos.com/sophos/docs/eng/marketing_material/sophos-threat-report-Q108.pdf) (PDF).
Sophos. Q1 2008. . Retrieved April 24, 2008.

[57] "Security threat report" (http://www.sophos.com/sophos/docs/eng/papers/sophos-security-report-jul08-srna.pdf) (PDF). Sophos. July
2008. . Retrieved August 24, 2008.

[58] Fogie, Seth, Jeremiah Grossman, Robert Hansen, and Anton Rager (2007) (PDF). *Cross Site Scripting Attacks: XSS Exploits and Defense*
(http://web.archive.org/web/20080625065121/http://www.syngress.com/book_catalog//SAMPLE_1597491543.pdf). Syngress,
Elsevier Science & Technology. pp. 68–69, 127. ISBN 1-59749-154-3. Archived from the original (http://www.syngress.com/
book catalog//SAMPLE_1597491543.pdf) on 2008-06-25. . Retrieved June 6, 2008.

[59] O'Reilly, Tim (September 30, 2005). "What Is Web 2.0" (http://www.oreillynet.com/pub/a/oreilly/tim/news/2005/09/30/
what-is-web-20.html). O'Reilly Media. pp. 4–5. . Retrieved June 4, 2008. and AJAX web applications can introduce security vulnerabilities
like "client-side security controls, increased attack surfaces, and new possibilities for Cross-Site Scripting (XSS)", in Ritchie, Paul (March
2007). "The security risks of AJAX/web 2.0 applications" (http://web.archive.org/web/20080625065122/http://www.
infosecurity-magazine.com/research/Sep07_Ajax.pdf) (PDF). *Infosecurity* (Elsevier). Archived from the original (http://www.
infosecurity-magazine.com/research/Sep07_Ajax.pdf) on 2008-06-25. . Retrieved June 6, 2008. which cites Hayre, Jaswinder S. and Kelath,
Jayasankar (June 22, 2006). "Ajax Security Basics" (http://www.securityfocus.com/infocus/1868). SecurityFocus. . Retrieved June 6,
2008.

[60] Berinato, Scott (January 1, 2007). "Software Vulnerability Disclosure: The Chilling Effect" (http://web.archive.org/web/
20080418072230/http://www.csoonline.com/article/221113). *CSO* (CXO Media): p. 7. Archived from the original (http://www.
csoonline.com/article/221113) on 2008-04-18. . Retrieved June 7, 2008.

[61] Prince, Brian (April 9, 2008). "McAfee Governance, Risk and Compliance Business Unit" (http://www.eweek.com/c/a/Security/
McAfee-Governance-Risk-and-Compliance-Business-Unit/). *eWEEK* (Ziff Davis Enterprise Holdings). . Retrieved April 25, 2008.

[62] Ben-Itzhak, Yuval (April 18, 2008). "Infosecurity 2008 – New defence strategy in battle against e-crime" (http://www.computerweekly.
com/Articles/2008/04/18/230345/infosecurity-2008-new-defence-strategy-in-battle-against.htm). *ComputerWeekly* (Reed Business
Information). . Retrieved April 20, 2008.

[63] Preston, Rob (April 12, 2008). "Down To Business: It's Past Time To Elevate The Infosec Conversation" (http://www.informationweek.
com/news/security/client/showArticle.jhtml?articleID=207100989). *InformationWeek* (United Business Media). . Retrieved April 25, 2008.

[64] Claburn, Thomas (February 6, 2007). "RSA's Coviello Predicts Security Consolidation" (http://www.informationweek.com/news/
security/showArticle.jhtml?articleID=197003826). *InformationWeek* (United Business Media). . Retrieved April 25, 2008.

[65] Duffy Marsan, Carolyn (April 9, 2008). "How the iPhone is killing the 'Net" (http://www.networkworld.com/news/2008/
040908-zittrain.html). *Network World* (IDG). . Retrieved April 17, 2008.

[66] "Web Accessibility Initiative (WAI)" (http://www.w3.org/WAI/l). World Wide Web Consortium. . Retrieved April 7, 2009.

[67] "Developing a Web Accessibility Business Case for Your Organization: Overview" (http://www.w3.org/WAI/bcase/Overview). World
Wide Web Consortium. . Retrieved April 7, 2009.

[68] "Legal and Policy Factors in Developing a Web Accessibility Business Case for Your Organization" (http://www.w3.org/WAI/bcase/
pol). World Wide Web Consortium. . Retrieved April 7, 2009.

[69] "Web Content Accessibility Guidelines (WCAG) Overview" (http://www.w3.org/WAI/intro/wcag.php). World Wide Web Consortium.
. Retrieved April 7, 2009.

[70] "Internationalization (I18n) Activity" (http://www.w3.org/International/). World Wide Web Consortium. . Retrieved April 10, 2009.

[71] Davis, Mark (April 5, 2008). "Moving to Unicode 5.1" (http://googleblog.blogspot.com/2008/05/moving-to-unicode-51.html). Google.
. Retrieved April 10, 2009.

[72] "World Wide Web Consortium Supports the IETF URI Standard and IRI Proposed Standard" (http://www.w3.org/2004/11/
uri-iri-pressrelease.html) (Press release). World Wide Web Consortium. January 26, 2005. . Retrieved April 10, 2009.

[73] Lynn, Jonathan (October 19, 2010). "Internet users to exceed 2 billion ..." (http://www.reuters.com/article/2010/10/19/
us-telecoms-internet-idUSTRE69I24720101019). Reuters. . Retrieved Feb 9, 2011.

[74] S. Lawrence, C.L. Giles, "Searching the World Wide Web," Science, 280(5360), 98-100, 1998.

[75] S. Lawrence, C.L. Giles, "Accessibility of Information on the Web," Nature, 400, 107-109, 1999.

[76] "The 'Deep' Web: Surfacing Hidden Value" (http://web.archive.org/web/20080404044203/http://www.brightplanet.com/resources/
details/deepweb.html). Brightplanet.com. Archived from the original (http://www.brightplanet.com/resources/details/deepweb.html) on
2008-04-04. . Retrieved July 27, 2009.

[77] "Distribution of languages on the Internet" (http://www.netz-tipp.de/languages.html). Netz-tipp.de. . Retrieved July 27, 2009.

[78] Alessio Signorini. "Indexable Web Size" (http://www.cs.uiowa.edu/~asignori/web-size/). Cs.uiowa.edu. . Retrieved July 27, 2009.

[79] "The size of the World Wide Web" (http://www.worldwidewebsize.com/). Worldwidewebsize.com. . Retrieved July 27, 2009.

[80] Alpert, Jesse; Hajaj, Nissan (July 25, 2008). "We knew the web was big..." (http://googleblog.blogspot.com/2008/07/
we-knew-web-was-big.html). *The Official Google Blog*. .

[81] "Domain Counts & Internet Statistics" (http://www.domaintools.com/internet-statistics/). Name Intelligence. . Retrieved May 17, 2009.

[82] "World Wide Wait" (http://www.techweb.com/encyclopedia/defineterm.jhtml?term=world+wide+wait). *TechEncyclopedia*. United
Business Media. . Retrieved April 10, 2009.

[83] Khare, Rohit and Jacobs, Ian (1999). "W3C Recommendations Reduce 'World Wide Wait'" (http://www.w3.org/Protocols/NL-PerfNote.
html). World Wide Web Consortium. . Retrieved April 10, 2009.

[84] Nielsen, Jakob (from Miller 1968; Card et al. 1991) (1994). "5" (http://www.useit.com/papers/responsetime.html). *Usability Engineering: Response Times: The Three Important Limits*. Morgan Kaufmann. . Retrieved April 10, 2009.

Further reading

- Niels Brügger, ed. *Web History* (2010) 362 pages; Historical perspective on the World Wide Web, including issues of culture, content, and preservation.
- Fielding, R.; Gettys, J.; Mogul, J.; Frystyk, H.; Masinter, L.; Leach, P.; Berners-Lee, T. (June 1999). *Hypertext Transfer Protocol — HTTP/1.1* (ftp://ftp.isi.edu/in-notes/rfc2616.txt). Request For Comments 2616. Information Sciences Institute.
- Berners-Lee, Tim; Bray, Tim; Connolly, Dan; Cotton, Paul; Fielding, Roy; Jeckle, Mario; Lilley, Chris; Mendelsohn, Noah; Orchard, David; Walsh, Norman; Williams, Stuart (December 15, 2004). *Architecture of the World Wide Web, Volume One* (http://www.w3.org/TR/webarch/). Version 20041215. W3C.
- Polo, Luciano (2003). "World Wide Web Technology Architecture: A Conceptual Analysis" (http://newdevices. com/publicaciones/www/). *New Devices*. Retrieved July 31, 2005.
- Skau, H.O. (March 1990). "The World Wide Web and Health Information" (http://newdevices.com/ publicaciones/www/). *New Devices*. Retrieved 1989.

External links

- Early archive of the first Web site (http://www.w3.org/History/19921103-hypertext/hypertext/WWW/)
- Internet Statistics: Growth and Usage of the Web and the Internet (http://www.mit.edu/people/mkgray/net/)
- Living Internet (http://www.livinginternet.com/w/w.htm) A comprehensive history of the Internet, including the World Wide Web.
- Web Design and Development (http://www.dmoz.org/Computers/Internet/Web_Design_and_Development/) at the Open Directory Project
- World Wide Web Consortium (W3C) (http://www.w3.org/)
- W3C Recommendations Reduce "World Wide Wait" (http://www.w3.org/Protocols/NL-PerfNote.html)
- World Wide Web Size (http://www.worldwidewebsize.com/) Daily estimated size of the World Wide Web.
- Antonio A. Casilli, Some Elements for a Sociology of Online Interactions (http://cle.ens-lyon.fr/40528325/0/ fiche___pagelibre/)
- The Erdős Webgraph Server (http://web-graph.org/) offers weekly updated graph representation of a constantly increasing fraction of the WWW.

Preferential_attachment

A **preferential attachment process** is any of a class of processes in which some quantity, typically some form of wealth or credit, is distributed among a number of individuals or objects according to how much they already have, so that those who are already wealthy receive more than those who are not. "Preferential attachment" is only the most recent of many names that have been given to such processes. They are also referred to under the names "Yule process", "cumulative advantage", "the rich get richer", and, less correctly, the "Matthew effect". It is related to Gibrat's law. The principal reason for scientific interest in preferential attachment is that it can, under suitable circumstances, generate power law distributions.

Definition

A preferential attachment process is a stochastic urn process, meaning a process in which discrete units of wealth, usually called "balls", are added in a random or partly random fashion to a set of objects or containers, usually called "urns". A preferential attachment process is an urn process in which additional balls are added continuously to the system and are distributed among the urns as an increasing function of the number of balls the urns already have. In the most commonly studied examples, the number of urns also increases continuously, although this is not a necessary condition for preferential attachment and examples have been studied with constant or even decreasing numbers of urns.

A classic example of a preferential attachment process is the growth in the number of species per genus in some higher taxon of biotic organisms.[1] New genera ("urns") are added to a taxon whenever a newly appearing species is considered sufficiently different from its predecessors that it does not belong in any of the current genera. New species ("balls") are added as old ones speciate (i.e., split in two) and, assuming that new species belong to the same genus as their parent (except for those that start new genera), the probability that a species is added to a new genus will be proportional to the number of species the genus already has. This process, first studied by Yule, is a *linear* preferential attachment process, since the rate at which genera accrue new species is linear in the number they already have.

Linear preferential attachment processes in which the number of urns increases are known to produce a distribution of balls over the urns following the so-called Yule distribution. In the most general form of the process, balls are added to the system at an overall rate of m new balls for each new urn. Each newly created urn starts out with k_0 balls and further balls are added to urns at a rate proportional to the number k that they already have plus a constant $a > -k_0$. With these definitions, the fraction $P(k)$ of urns having k balls in the limit of long time is given by[2]

for $k \geq k_0$ (and zero otherwise), where $B(x, y)$ is the Euler beta function:

with $\Gamma(x)$ being the standard gamma function, and

The beta function behaves asymptotically as $B(x, y) \sim x^{-y}$ for large x and fixed y, which implies that for large values of k we have

In other words, the preferential attachment process generates a "long-tailed" distribution following a Pareto distribution or power law in its tail. This is the primary reason for the historical interest in preferential attachment: the species distribution and many other phenomena are observed empirically to follow power laws and the preferential attachment process is a leading candidate mechanism to explain this behavior. Preferential attachment is considered a possible candidate for, among other things, the distribution of the sizes of cities,[3] the wealth of extremely wealthy individuals,[3] the number of citations received by learned publications,[4] and the number of links to pages on the World Wide Web.[5]

The general model described here includes many other specific models as special cases. In the species/genus example above, for instance, each genus starts out with a single species ($k_0 = 1$) and gains new species in direct proportion to the number it already has ($a = 0$), and hence $P(k) = B(k, \gamma)/B(k_0, \gamma - 1)$ with $\gamma = 2 + 1/m$. Similarly the

Price model for scientific citations[4] corresponds to the case $k_0 = 0$, $a = 1$ and the widely studied Barabási-Albert model[5] corresponds to $k_0 = m$, $a = 0$.

Preferential attachment is sometimes referred to as the Matthew effect, but the two are not precisely equivalent. The Matthew effect, first discussed by Robert Merton,[6] is named for a passage in the biblical Gospel of Matthew: "For everyone who has will be given more, and he will have an abundance. Whoever does not have, even what he has will be taken from him." (Matthew 25:29, New International Version.) The preferential attachment process does not incorporate the taking away part. An urn process that includes both the giving and the taking away would produce a log-normal distribution rather than a power law . This point may be moot, however, since the scientific insight behind the Matthew effect is in any case entirely different. Qualitatively it is intended to describe not a mechanical multiplicative effect like preferential attachment but a specific human behavior in which people are more likely to give credit to the famous than to the little known. The classic example of the Matthew effect is a scientific discovery made simultaneously by two different people, one well known and the other little known. It is claimed that under these circumstances people tend more often to credit the discovery to the well-known scientist. Thus the real-world phenomenon the Matthew effect is intended to describe is quite distinct from (though certainly related to) preferential attachment.

History

The first rigorous consideration of preferential attachment seems to be that of Yule in 1925, who used it to explain the power-law distribution of the number of species per genus of flowering plants.[1] The process is sometimes called a "Yule process" in his honor. Yule was able to show that the process gave rise to a distribution with a power-law tail, but the details of his proof are, by today's standards, contorted and difficult, since the modern tools of stochastic process theory did not yet exist and he was forced to use more cumbersome methods of proof.

Most modern treatments of preferential attachment make use of the master equation method, whose use in this context was pioneered by Simon in 1955, in work on the distribution of sizes of cities and other phenomena.[3]

The first application of preferential attachment to learned citations was given by Price in 1976.[4] (He referred to the process as a "cumulative advantage" process.) His was also the first application of the process to the growth of a network, producing what would now be called a scale-free network. It is in the context of network growth that the process is most frequently studied today. Price also promoted preferential attachment as a possible explanation for power laws in many other phenomena, including Lotka's law of scientific productivity and Bradford's law of journal use.

The application of preferential attachment to the growth of the World Wide Web was proposed by Barabási and Albert in 1999.[5] Barabási and Albert also coined the name "preferential attachment" by which the process is best known today and suggested that the process might apply to the growth of other networks as well.

See also

- Assortative mixing
- Stochastic processes
- Power law
- Yule–Simon distribution
- Simon model
- Complex network
- BA model
- Wealth condensation
- Chinese restaurant process
- Bose–Einstein condensation: a network theory approach

- Double jeopardy (marketing)
- Capital accumulation
- Wealth condensation
- The rich get richer and the poor get poorer
- Matthew effect (sociology)

References

[1] Yule, G. U. (1925). "A Mathematical Theory of Evolution, based on the Conclusions of Dr. J. C. Willis, F.R.S". *Philosophical Transactions of the Royal Society of London, Ser. B* **213** (402–410): 21–87. doi:10.1098/rstb.1925.0002.

[2] Newman, M. E. J. (2005). "Power laws, Pareto distributions and Zipf's law". *Contemporary Physics* **46** (5): 323–351. arXiv:cond-mat/0412004. doi:10.1080/00107510500052444.

[3] Simon, H. A. (1955). "On a class of skew distribution functions". *Biometrika* **42** (3–4): 425–440. doi:10.1093/biomet/42.3-4.425.

[4] Price, D. J. de S. (1976). "A general theory of bibliometric and other cumulative advantage processes" (http://garfield.library.upenn.edu/price/pricetheory1976.pdf). *J. Amer. Soc. Inform. Sci.* **27** (5): 292–306. doi:10.1002/asi.4630270505. .

[5] Barabási, A.-L.; R. Albert (1999). "Emergence of scaling in random networks". *Science* **286** (5439): 509–512. arXiv:cond-mat/9910332. doi:10.1126/science.286.5439.509.

[6] Merton, Robert K. (1968). "The Matthew effect in science". *Science* **159** (3810): 56–63. doi:10.1126/science.159.3810.56. PMID 17737466.

Degree_distribution

In the study of graphs and networks, the degree of a node in a network is the number of connections it has to other nodes and the **degree distribution** is the probability distribution of these degrees over the whole network.

Definition

The degree of a node in a network (sometimes referred to incorrectly as the connectivity) is the number of connections or edges the node has to other nodes. If a network is directed, meaning that edges point in one direction from one node to another

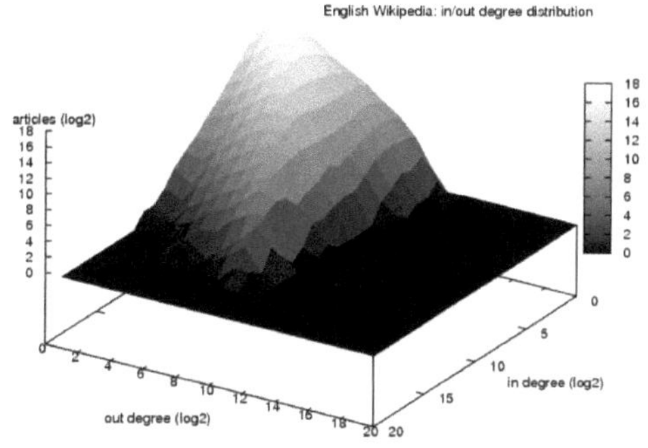

In/out degree distribution for Wikipedia's hyperlink graph (logarithmic scales)

node, then nodes have two different degrees, the in-degree, which is the number of incoming edges, and the out-degree, which is the number of outgoing edges.

The degree distribution $P(k)$ of a network is then defined to be the fraction of nodes in the network with degree k. Thus if there are n nodes in total in a network and n_k of them have degree k, we have $P(k) = n_k/n$.

The same information is also sometimes presented in the form of a *cumulative degree distribution*, the fraction of nodes with degree greater than or equal to k.

Observed degree distributions

The degree distribution is very important in studying both real networks, such as the Internet and social networks, and theoretical networks. The simplest network model, for example, the (Bernoulli) random graph, in which each of n nodes is connected (or not) with independent probability p (or $1 - p$), has a binomial distribution of degrees:

(or Poisson in the limit of large n). Most networks in the real world, however, have degree distributions very different from this. Most are highly right-skewed, meaning that a large majority of nodes have low degree but a small number, known as "hubs", have high degree. Some networks, notably the Internet, the world wide web, and some social networks are found to have degree distributions that approximately follow a power law: $P(k) \sim k^{-\gamma}$, where γ is a constant. Such networks are called scale-free networks and have attracted particular attention for their structural and dynamical properties.

See also

- Graph theory
- Complex network
- Scale-free network
- Random graph

References

- Albert, R.; Barabasi, A.-L. (2002). "Statistical mechanics of complex networks". *Reviews of Modern Physics* **74**: 47–97. arXiv:cond-mat/0106096. Bibcode 2002RvMP...74...47A. doi:10.1103/RevModPhys.74.47.
- Dorogovtsev, S.; Mendes, J. F. F. (2002). "Evolution of networks". *Advances in Physics* **51** (4): 1079–1187. arXiv:cond-mat/0106144. doi:10.1080/00018730110112519.
- Newman, M. E. J. (2003). "The structure and function of complex networks" [1]. *SIAM Review* **45** (2): 167–256. doi:10.1137/S003614450342480.
- Shlomo Havlin and Reuven Cohen (2010). *Complex Networks: Structure, Robustness and Function* [2]. Cambridge University Press.

References

[1] http://siamdl.aip.org/getabs/servlet/GetabsServlet?prog=normal&id=SIREAD000045000002000167000001
[2] http://havlin.biu.ac.il/Shlomo%20Havlin%20books_com_net.php

Power_law

A **power law** is a mathematical relationship between two quantities. When the frequency of an event varies as a power of some attribute of that event (e.g. its size), the frequency is said to follow a power law. For instance, the number of cities having a certain population size is found to vary as a power of the size of the population, and hence follows a power law. There is evidence that the distributions of a wide variety of physical, biological, and man-made phenomena follow a power law, including the sizes of earthquakes, craters on the moon and of solar flares,[1] the

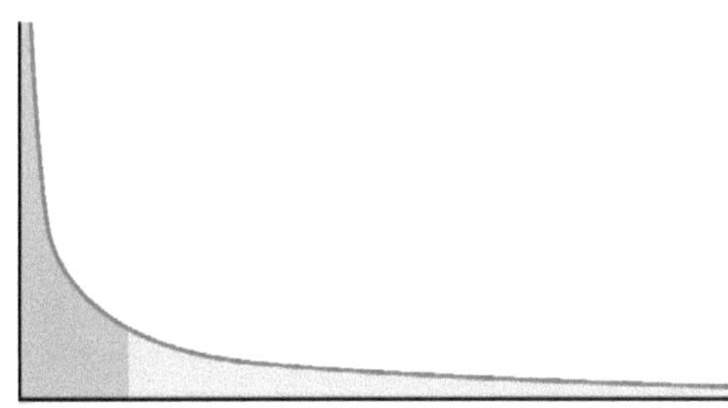

An example power-law graph, being used to demonstrate ranking of popularity. To the right is the long tail, and to the left are the few that dominate (also known as the 80-20 rule).

foraging pattern of various species,[2] the sizes of activity patterns of neuronal populations,[3] the frequencies of words in most languages, frequencies of family names, the species richness in clades of organisms,[4] the sizes of power outages and wars,[5] and many other quantities.

Properties of power laws

Scale invariance

The main property of power laws that makes them interesting is their scale invariance. Given a relation , scaling the argument by a constant factor causes only a proportionate scaling of the function itself. That is,

That is, scaling by a constant simply multiplies the original power-law relation by the constant . Thus, it follows that all power laws with a particular scaling exponent are equivalent up to constant factors, since each is simply a scaled version of the others. This behavior is what produces the linear relationship when logarithms are taken of both and , and the straight-line on the log-log plot is often called the *signature* of a power law. With real data, such straightness is a necessary, but not sufficient, condition for the data following a power-law relation. In fact, there are many ways to generate finite amounts of data that mimic this signature behavior, but, in their asymptotic limit, are not true power laws. Thus, accurately fitting and validating power-law models is an active area of research in statistics.

Universality

The equivalence of power laws with a particular scaling exponent can have a deeper origin in the dynamical processes that generate the power-law relation. In physics, for example, phase transitions in thermodynamic systems are associated with the emergence of power-law distributions of certain quantities, whose exponents are referred to as the critical exponents of the system. Diverse systems with the same critical exponents—that is, which display identical scaling behaviour as they approach criticality—can be shown, via renormalization group theory, to share the same fundamental dynamics. For instance, the behavior of water and CO_2 at their boiling points fall in the same universality class because they have identical critical exponents. In fact, almost all material phase transitions are described by a small set of universality classes. Similar observations have been made, though not as comprehensively, for various self-organized critical systems, where the critical point of the system is an attractor. Formally, this sharing of dynamics is referred to as universality, and systems with precisely the same critical exponents are said to belong to the same universality class.

Power-law functions

The general power-law function follows the polynomial form given above, and is a ubiquitous form throughout mathematics and science. Notably, however, not all polynomial functions are power laws because not all polynomials exhibit the property of scale invariance. Typically, power-law functions are polynomials in a single variable, and are explicitly used to model the scaling behavior of natural processes. For instance, allometric scaling laws for the relation of biological variables are some of the best known power-law functions in nature. In this context, the term is most typically replaced by a deviation term , which can represent uncertainty in the observed values (perhaps measurement or sampling errors) or provide a simple way for observations to deviate from the power-law function (perhaps for stochastic reasons):

Scientific interest in power law relations stems partly from the ease with which certain general classes of mechanisms generate them (see the Sornette reference below). The demonstration of a power-law relation in some data can point to specific kinds of mechanisms that might underlie the natural phenomenon in question, and can indicate a deep connection with other, seemingly unrelated systems (see the reference by Simon and the subsection on universality below). The ubiquity of power-law relations in physics is partly due to dimensional constraints, while in complex systems, power laws are often thought to be signatures of hierarchy or of specific stochastic processes. A few notable examples of power laws are the Gutenberg-Richter law for earthquake sizes, Pareto's law of income distribution, structural self-similarity of fractals, and scaling laws in biological systems. Research on the origins of power-law relations, and efforts to observe and validate them in the real world, is an active topic of research in many fields of science, including physics, computer science, linguistics, geophysics, neuroscience, sociology, economics and more.

However much of the recent interest in power laws comes from the study of probability distributions: it's now known that the distributions of a wide variety of quantities seem to follow the power-law form, at least in their upper tail (large events). The behavior of these large events connects these quantities to the study of theory of large deviations (also called extreme value theory), which considers the frequency of extremely rare events like stock market crashes and large natural disasters. It is primarily in the study of statistical distributions that the name "power law" is used; in other areas the power-law functional form is more often referred to simply as a polynomial form or polynomial function.

Examples of power-law functions

- The Stevens' power law of psychophysics
- The Stefan–Boltzmann law
- The Ramberg–Osgood stress–strain relationship
- The input-voltage–output-current curves of field-effect transistors and vacuum tubes approximate a square-law relationship, a factor in "tube sound".
- A 3/2-power law can be found in the plate characteristic curves of triodes.
- The inverse-square laws of Newtonian gravity and electrostatics
- Electrostatic potential and gravitational potential
- Model of van der Waals force
- Force and potential in simple harmonic motion
- Kepler's third law
- The initial mass function of stars
- The M-sigma relation
- Gamma correction relating light intensity with voltage
- Kleiber's law relating animal metabolism to size, and allometric laws in general
- Behaviour near second-order phase transitions involving critical exponents
- Proposed form of experience curve effects

- The differential energy spectrum of cosmic-ray nuclei
- Square-cube law (ratio of surface area to volume)
- Constructal law
- Fractals
- The Pareto principle also called the "80–20 rule"
- Zipf's law in corpus analysis and population distributions amongst others, where frequency of an item or event is inversely proportional to its frequency rank (i.e. the second most frequent item/event occurring half as often the most frequent item and so on).
- The safe operating area relating to maximum simultaneous current and voltage in power semiconductors.
- The unequal participation and traffic in relation to the use of communications tools as noted by Clay Shirky in Here Comes Everybody.

Variants

Broken power law

A broken power law is defined with a threshold:

$$\text{for },$$

$$\text{for }.$$

Power law with exponential cutoff

A power law with an exponential cutoff is simply a power law multiplied by an exponential function:

Curved power law

Power-law probability distributions

In the most general sense, a power-law probability distribution is a distribution whose density function (or mass function in the discrete case) has the form

where , and is a **slowly varying function**, which is any function that satisfies with constant. This property of follows directly from the requirement that be asymptotically scale invariant; thus, the form of only controls the shape and finite extent of the lower tail. For instance, if is the constant function, then we have a power-law that holds for all values of . In many cases, it is convenient to assume a lower bound from which the law holds. Combining these two cases, and where is a continuous variable, the power law has the form

where the pre-factor to is the normalizing constant. We can now consider several properties of this distribution. For instance, its moments are given by

which is only well defined for . That is, all moments diverge: when , the average and all higher-order moments are infinite; when , the mean exists, but the variance and higher-order moments are infinite, etc. For finite-size samples drawn from such distribution, this behavior implies that the central moment estimators (like the mean and the variance) for diverging moments will never converge - as more data is accumulated, they continue to grow. These power-law probability distributions are also called Pareto-type distributions, distributions with Pareto tails, or distributions with regularly varying tails.

Another kind of power-law distribution, which does not satisfy the general form above, is the power law with an exponential cutoff

In this distribution, the exponential decay term eventually overwhelms the power-law behavior at very large values of . This distribution does not scale and is thus not asymptotically a power law; however, it does approximately scale over a finite region before the cutoff. (Note that the pure form above is a subset of this family, with .) This distribution is a common alternative to the asymptotic power-law distribution because it naturally captures finite-size effects. For instance, although the Gutenberg–Richter law is commonly cited as an example of a power-law distribution, the distribution of earthquake magnitudes cannot scale as a power law in the limit because there is a finite amount of energy in the Earth's crust and thus there must be some maximum size to an earthquake. As the scaling behavior approaches this size, it must taper off.

Graphical methods for the identification of power-law probability distributions from random samples

Although more sophisticated and robust methods have been proposed, the most frequently used graphical methods of identifying power-law probability distributions using random samples are Pareto quantile-quantile plots (or Pareto Q-Q plots), mean residual life plots (see, e.g., the books by Beirlant et al.[6] and Coles [7]) and log-log plots. Another, more robust graphical method uses bundles of residual quantile functions.[8] (Please keep in mind that power-law distributions are also called Pareto-type distributions.) It is assumed here that a random sample is obtained from a probability distribution, and that we want to know if the tail of the distribution follows a power-law (in other words, we want to know if the distribution has a "Pareto tail"). Here, the random sample is called "the data".

Pareto Q-Q plots compare the quantiles of the log-transformed data to the corresponding quantiles of an exponential distribution with mean 1 (or to the quantiles of a standard Pareto distribution) by plotting the former versus the latter. If the resultant scatterplot suggests that the plotted points " asymptotically converge" to a straight line, then a power-law distribution should be suspected. A limitation of Pareto Q-Q plots is that they behave poorly when the tail index (also called Pareto index) is close to 0, because Pareto Q-Q plots are not designed to identify distributions with slowly varying tails.[8]

On the other hand, in its version for identifying power-law probability distributions, the mean residual life plot consists of first log-transforming the data, and then plotting the average of those log-transformed data that are higher than the i-th order statistic versus the i-th order statistic, for all i=1,...,n, where n is the size of the random sample. If the resultant scatterplot suggests that the plotted points tend to "stabilize" about a horizontal straight line, then a power-law distribution should be suspected. Since the mean residual life plot is very sensitive to outliers (it is not robust), it usually produces plots that are difficult to interpret; for this reason, such plots are usually called Hill horror plots [9]

Log-log plots are an alternative way of graphically examining the tail of a distribution using a random sample. This method consists of plotting the logarithm of an estimator of the probability that a particular number of the distribution occurs versus the logarithm of that particular number. Usually, this estimator is the proportion of times that the number occurs in the data set. If the points in the plot tend to "converge" to a straight line for large numbers in the x axis, then the researcher concludes that the distribution has a power-law tail. An example of the application of these types of plot can be found, for instance, in Jeong et al.[10] A disadvantage of this plots is that, in order for them to provide reliable results, they require huge amounts of data. In addition, they are appropriate only for discrete (or grouped) data.

Another graphical method for the identification of power-law probability distributions using random samples has been proposed.[8] This methodology consists of plotting a *bundle for the log-transformed sample*. Originally proposed as a tool to explore the existence of moments and the moment generation function using random samples, the bundle methodology is based on residual quantile functions (RQFs), also called residual percentile functions,[11] [12] [13] [14] [15] [16] [17] which provide a full characterization of the tail behavior of many well-known probability distributions, including power-law distributions, distributions with other types of heavy tails, and even non-heavy-tailed distributions. Bundle plots do not have the disadvantages of Pareto Q-Q plots, mean residual life plots and log-log plots mentioned above (they are robust to outliers, allow visually identifying power-laws with small values of , and do not demand the collection of much data). In addition, other types of tail behavior can be identified using bundle plots.

Plotting power-law distributions

In general, power-law distributions are plotted on doubly logarithmic axes, which emphasizes the upper tail region. The most convenient way to do this is via the (complementary) cumulative distribution (cdf), ,

Note that the cdf is also a power-law function, but with a smaller scaling exponent. For data, an equivalent form of the cdf is the rank-frequency approach, in which we first sort the observed values in ascending order, and plot them against the vector .

Although it can be convenient to log-bin the data, or otherwise smooth the probability density (mass) function directly, these methods introduce an implicit bias in the representation of the data, and thus should be avoided. The cdf, on the other hand, introduces no bias in the data and preserves the linear signature on doubly logarithmic axes.

Estimating the exponent from empirical data

There are many ways of estimating the value of the scaling exponent for a power-law tail, however not all of them yield unbiased and consistent answers. Some of the most reliable techniques are often based on the method of maximum likelihood. Alternative methods are often based on making a linear regression on either the log-log probability, the log-log cumulative distribution function, or on log-binned data, but these approaches should be avoided as they can all lead to highly biased estimates of the scaling exponent (see the Clauset et al. reference below).

Maximum likelihood

For real-valued, independent and identically distributed data, we fit a power-law distribution of the form

to the data , where the coefficient is included to ensure that the distribution is normalized. Given a choice for , a simple derivation by this method yields the estimator equation

where are the data points . (For a more detailed derivation, see Hall or Newman below.) This estimator exhibits a small finite sample-size bias of order , which is small when $n > 100$. Further, the uncertainty in the estimation can be derived from the maximum likelihood argument, and has the form . This estimator is equivalent to the popular Hill estimator from quantitative finance and extreme value theory.

For a set of n integer-valued data points , again where each , the maximum likelihood exponent is the solution to the transcendental equation

where is the incomplete zeta function. The uncertainty in this estimate follows the same formula as for the continuous equation. However, the two equations for are not equivalent, and the continuous version should not be applied to discrete data, nor vice versa.

Further, both of these estimators require the choice of . For functions with a non-trivial function, choosing too small produces a significant bias in , while choosing it too large increases the uncertainty in , and reduces the statistical power of our model. In general, the best choice of depends strongly on the particular form of the lower tail, represented by above.

More about these methods, and the conditions under which they can be used, can be found in the Clauset et al. reference below. Further, this comprehensive review article provides usable code [18] (Matlab, R and C++) for estimation and testing routines for power-law distributions.

Kolmogorov–Smirnov estimation

Another method for the estimation of the power law exponent, which does not assume independent and identically distributed (iid) data, uses the minimization of the Kolmogorov–Smirnov statistic, , between the cumulative distribution functions of the data and the power law:

with

where and denote the cdfs of the data and the power law with exponent , respectively. As this method does not assume iid data, it provides an alternative way to determine the power law exponent for data sets in which the temporal correlation can not be ignored.[3]

Two point fitting method

This criterion can be applied for the estimation of power law exponent in the case of scale free distributions and provides a more convergent estimate than the maximum likelihood method. The method is described in Guerriero et al. (2011) where it has been applied to study probability distributions of fracture aperture. In some contexts the probability distribution is described, not by the cumulative distribution function, by the cumulative frequency of a property X, defined as the number of elements per meter (or area unit, second etc.) for which $X > x$ applies, where x is a variable real number. As an example, the cumulative distribution of the fracture aperture, X, for a sample of N elements is defined as 'the number of fractures per meter having aperture greater than x '. Use of cumulative frequency has some advantages, e.g. it allows one to put on the same diagram data gathered from sample lines of different lengths at different scales (e.g. from outcrop and from microscope).

Examples of power-law distributions

- Pareto distribution (continuous)
- Zeta distribution (discrete)
- Yule–Simon distribution (discrete)
- Student's t-distribution (continuous), of which the Cauchy distribution is a special case
- Zipf's law and its generalization, the Zipf–Mandelbrot law (discrete)
  - Lotka's law
- The scale-free network model
- Bibliograms
- Neuronal avalanches[3]
- Horton's laws describing river systems
- Richardson's Law for the severity of violent conflicts (wars and terrorism)
- Population of cities
- Numbers of religious adherents
- Frequency of words in a text
- Pink noise
- 90–9–1 principle on wikis

A great many power-law distributions have been conjectured in recent years. For instance, power laws are thought to characterize the behavior of the upper tails for the popularity of websites, the degree distribution of the webgraph, describing the hyperlink structure of the WWW, the net worth of individuals, the number of species per genus, the popularity of given names, Gutenberg–Richter law of earthquake magnitudes, the size of financial returns, and many others. However, much debate remains as to which of these tails are actually power-law distributed and which are not. For instance, it is commonly accepted now that the famous Gutenberg–Richter law decays more rapidly than a pure power-law tail because of a finite exponential cutoff in the upper tail.

Validating power laws

Although power-law relations are attractive for many theoretical reasons, demonstrating that data do indeed follow a power-law relation requires more than simply fitting a particular model to the data. In general, many alternative functional forms can appear to follow a power-law form for some extent (see the Laherrere and Sornette reference below). Also, researchers usually have to face the problem of deciding whether or not a real-world probability distribution follows a power law. As a solution to this problem, Diaz[8] proposed a graphical methodology based on random samples that allow visually discerning between different types of tail behavior. This methodology uses bundles of residual quantile functions, also called percentile residual life functions, which characterize many different types of distribution tails, including both heavy and non-heavy tails.

A method for validation of power-law relations is by testing many orthogonal predictions of a particular generative mechanism against data. Simply fitting a power-law relation to a particular kind of data is not considered a rational approach. As such, the validation of power-law claims remains a very active field of research in many areas of modern science.[5]

See also

- Empirical relationship
- Fat tail
- Finite-time singularity
- Fractional dynamics
- Heavy-tailed distributions
- Hyperbolic growth
- Lévy flight
- Lognormal distribution
- Long Tail

- Power law fluid
- Simon model
- stable distribution
- Stevens' power law
- Wealth condensation
- Allometric law
- Extreme value theory
- Kleiber's law
- Zipf's law
- Webgraph

Notes

[1] Newman, M. E. J. (2005). "Power laws, Pareto distributions and Zipf's law". *Contemporary Physics* **46** (5): 323–351. doi:10.1080/00107510500052444.

[2] Humphries NE, Queiroz N, Dyer JR, Pade NG, Musyl MK, Schaefer KM, Fuller DW, Brunnschweiler JM, Doyle TK, Houghton JD, Hays GC, Jones CS, Noble LR, Wearmouth VJ, Southall EJ, Sims DW (2010). "Environmental context explains Lévy and Brownian movement patterns of marine predators". *Nature* **465** (7301): 1066–1069. doi:10.1038/nature09116. PMID 20531470.

[3] Klaus A, Yu S, Plenz D (2011). Zochowski, Michal. ed. "Statistical Analyses Support Power Law Distributions Found in Neuronal Avalanches" (http://www.plosone.org/article/info:doi/10.1371/journal.pone.0019779). *PLoS ONE* **6** (5): e19779. doi:10.1371/journal.pone.0019779. PMC 3102672. PMID 21720544. .

[4] Albert, J. S.; Reis, R. E., eds. (2011). *Historical Biogeography of Neotropical Freshwater Fishes* (http://www.ucpress.edu/book. php?isbn=9780520268685). Berkeley: University of California Press. .

[5] Aaron Clauset, Cosma Rohilla Shalizi, M. E. J. Newman (2009). "Power-law distributions in empirical data". *SIAM Review* **51** (4): 661–703. arXiv:0706.1062v2. doi:10.1137/070710111.

[6] Beirlant, J., Teugels, J. L., Vynckier, P. (1996a), Practical Analysis of Extreme Values, Leuven: Leuven University Press

[7] Coles, S. (2001) An introduction to statistical modeling of extreme values. Springer-Verlag, London.

[8] Diaz F. J. (1999). "Identifying Tail Behavior by Means of Residual Quantile Functions". *Journal of Computational and Graphical Statistics* **8** (3): 493–509. doi:10.2307/1390871.

[9] Resnick, S. I. (1997), Heavy Tail Modeling and TeΔletraffic Data, The Annals of Statistics, 25, 1805-1869.

[10] Jeong H, Tombor B. Albert, Oltvai Z.N., Barabasi A.-L. (2000). "The large-scale organization of metabolic networks". *Nature* **407** (6804): 651–654. doi:10.1038/35036627. PMID 11034217.

[11] Arnold, B. C., Brockett, P. L. (1983), When does the βth percentile residual life function determine the distribution?, Operations Research 31, no. 2, Operations Research Society of America, 391–396.

[12] Joe, H., Proschan, F. (1984), Percentile residual life functions, Operations Research 32, no. 3, Operations Research Society of America, 668–678.

[13] Joe, H. (1985), Characterizations of life distributions from percentile residual lifetimes, Ann. Inst. Statist. Math. 37, Part A, 165–172.

[14] Csorgo, S., Viharos, L. (1992), Confidence bands for percentile residual lifetimes, Journal of Statistical Planning and Inference 30, North-Holland, 327–337.

[15] Schmittlein, D. C., Morrison, D. G. (1981), The median residual lifetime: A characterization theorem and an application, Operations Research 29, no. 2, Operations Research Society of America, 392–399.

[16] Morrison, D. G., Schmittlein, D. C. (1980), Jobs, strikes, and wars: Probability models for duration, Organizational Behavior and Human Performance 25, Academic Press, Inc., 224–251.

[17] Gerchak, Y. (1984), Decreasing failure rates and related issues in the social sciences, Operations Research 32, no. 3, Operations Research Society of America, 537–546.

[18] http://www.santafe.edu/~aaronc/powerlaws/

Bibliography

- Clauset, A., Shalizi, C. R. and Newman, M. E. J. (2009). "Power-law distributions in empirical data". *SIAM Review* **51** (4): 661–703. arXiv:0706.1062. doi:10.1137/070710111.

- V. Guerriero, S. Vitale, S. Ciarcia, S. Mazzoli (2011). "Improved statistical multi-scale analysis of fractures in carbonate reservoir analogues". *Tectonophysics* (Elsevier) **504**: 14–24. doi:10.1016/j.tecto.2011.01.003.

- Hall, P. (1982). "On Some Simple Estimates of an Exponent of Regular Variation". *Journal of the Royal Statistical Society, Series B (Methodological)* **44** (1): 37–42. JSTOR 2984706.

- Laherrere, J. and D. Sornette (1998). "Stretched exponential distributions in Nature and Economy: 'Fat tails' with characteristic scales". *European Physical Journal B* **2** (4): 525–539. arXiv:cond-mat/9801293. doi:10.1007/s100510050276.

- Mitzenmacher, M. (2003). "A brief history of generative models for power law and lognormal distributions" (http://www.internetmathematics.org/volumes/1/2/pp226_251.pdf). *Internet Mathematics* **1**: 226–251.

- Newman, M. E. J. (2005). "Power laws, Pareto distributions and Zipf's law". *Contemporary Physics* **46** (5): 323–351. arXiv:cond-mat/0412004. doi:10.1080/00107510500052444.

- "Theory of Zipf's law and beyond", Alexander Saichev, Yannick Malevergne and Didier Sornette (2009) Lecture Notes in Economics and Mathematical Systems, Volume 632, Springer (November 2009), ISBN 978-3-642-02945-5

- Simon, H. A. (1955). "On a Class of Skew Distribution Functions". *Biometrika* **42** (3/4): 425–440. doi:10.2307/2333389. JSTOR 2333389.

- *Critical Phenomena in Natural Sciences (Chaos, Fractals, Self-organization and Disorder: Concepts and Tools),* Didier Sornette (2006) 2nd ed., 2nd print (Springer Series in Synergetics, Heidelberg).

- *Ubiquity* Mark Buchanan (2000) Wiedenfield & Nicholson ISBN 0 297 64376 2

- Stumpf, M.P.H. and Porter, M.A. "Critical Truths about Power Laws" *Science* **2012**, 335, 665-6

External links

- Zipf's law (http://www.nslij-genetics.org/wli/zipf/)
- Zipf, Power-laws, and Pareto - a ranking tutorial (http://www.hpl.hp.com/research/idl/papers/ranking/ranking.html)
- Gutenberg-Richter Law (http://simscience.org/crackling/Advanced/Earthquakes/GutenbergRichter.html)
- Stream Morphometry and Horton's Laws (http://www.physicalgeography.net/fundamentals/10ab.html)
- Clay Shirky on Institutions & Collaboration: Power law in relation to the internet-based social networks (http://www.youtube.com/watch?v=sPQViNNOAkw)
- Clay Shirky on Power Laws, Weblogs, and Inequality (http://shirky.com/writings/powerlaw_weblog.html)
- "How the Finance Gurus Get Risk All Wrong" (http://www.fooledbyrandomness.com/fortune.pdf) by Benoit Mandelbrot & Nassim Nicholas Taleb. *Fortune*, July 11, 2005.
- "Million-dollar Murray": (http://www.newyorker.com/fact/content/articles/060213fa_fact) power-law distributions in homelessness and other social problems; by Malcolm Gladwell. *The New Yorker*, February 13,

2006.

- Benoit Mandelbrot & Richard Hudson: The Misbehaviour of Markets (2004)
- Philip Ball: Critical Mass: How one thing leads to another (http://www.agrfoto.com/philipball/criticalmass. php) (2005)
- *Tyranny of the Power Law* (http://econophysics.blogspot.com/2006/07/ tyranny-of-power-law-and-why-we-should.html) from The Econophysics Blog (http://econophysics.blogspot. com)
- *So You Think You Have a Power Law — Well Isn't That Special?* (http://www.cscs.umich.edu/~crshalizi/ weblog/491.html) from Three-Toed Sloth (http://www.cscs.umich.edu/~crshalizi/weblog/), the blog of Cosma Shalizi, Professor of Statistics at Carnegie-Mellon University.
- Simple MATLAB script (http://www.mathworks.com/matlabcentral/fileexchange/27176-log-binning-of-data) which bins data to illustrate power-law distributions (if any) in the data.
- The Erdős Webgraph Server (http://web-graph.org) visualizes the distribution of the degrees of the webgraph on the download page (http://web-graph.org/index.php/download).

Probability_distribution

In probability theory, a **probability mass**, **probability density**, or **probability distribution** is a function that describes the probability of a random variable taking certain values.

For a more precise definition one needs to distinguish between **discrete** and **continuous** random variables. In the discrete case, one can easily assign a probability to each possible value: when throwing a die, each of the six values *1* to *6* has the probability 1/6. In contrast, when a random variable takes values from a continuum, probabilities are nonzero only if they refer to finite intervals: in quality control one might demand that the probability of a "500 g" package containing between 490 g and 510 g should be no less than 98%.

If a total order is defined for the random variable, the **cumulative distribution function** gives the probability that the random variable is no larger than a given value; it is the integral of the non-cumulative distribution.

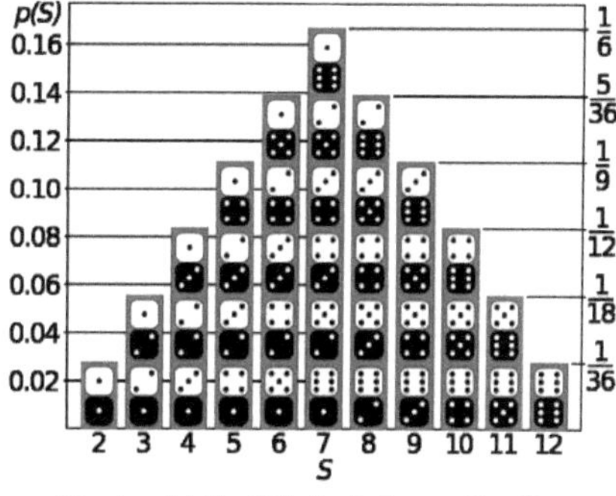

Terminology

As probability theory is used in quite diverse applications, terminology is not uniform and sometimes confusing. The following terms are used for non-cumulative probability distribution functions:

- **Probability mass, Probability mass function, p.m.f.**: for discrete random variables.
- **Categorical distribution**: for discrete random variables with a finite set of values.

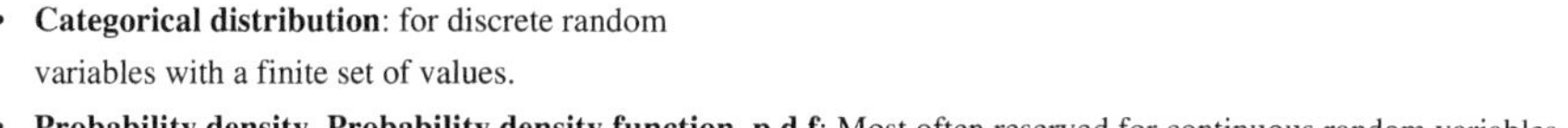

Discrete probability distribution for the sum of two dice.

- **Probability density, Probability density function, p.d.f**: Most often reserved for continuous random variables.

The following terms are somewhat ambiguous as they can refer to non-cumulative or cumulative distributions, depending on authors' preferences:

- **Probability distribution function**: Continuous or discrete, non-cumulative or cumulative.
- **Probability function**: Even more ambiguous, can mean any of the above, or anything else.

Finally,

- **Probability distribution**: Either the same as *probability distribution function*. Or understood as something more fundamental underlying an actual mass or density function.

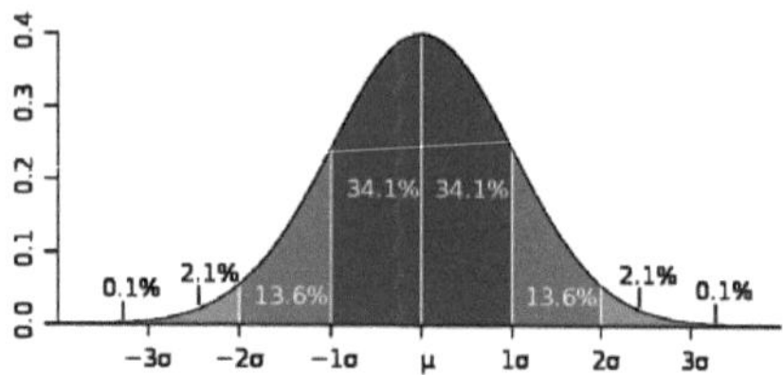

Normal distribution, also called Gaussian or "bell curve", the most important continuous random distribution.

Basic terms

- **Mode**: most frequently occurring value in a distribution
- **Tail**: region of least frequently occurring values in a distribution

Discrete probability distribution

A **discrete probability distribution** shall be understood as a *probability distribution* characterized by a probability mass function. Thus, the distribution of a random variable X is discrete, and X is then called a **discrete random variable**, if

as u runs through the set of all possible values of X. It follows that such a random variable can assume only a finite or countably infinite number of values.

In cases more frequently considered, this set of possible values is a topologically discrete set in the sense that all its points are isolated points. But there are discrete random variables for which this countable set is dense on the real line (for example, a distribution over rational numbers).

Among the most well-known discrete probability distributions that are used for statistical modeling are the Poisson distribution, the Bernoulli distribution, the binomial distribution, the geometric distribution, and the negative binomial distribution. In addition, the discrete uniform distribution is commonly used in computer programs that make equal-probability random selections between a number of choices.

The probability mass function of a discrete probability distribution. The probabilities of the singletons {1}, {3}, and {7} are respectively 0.2, 0.5, 0.3. A set not containing any of these points has probability zero.

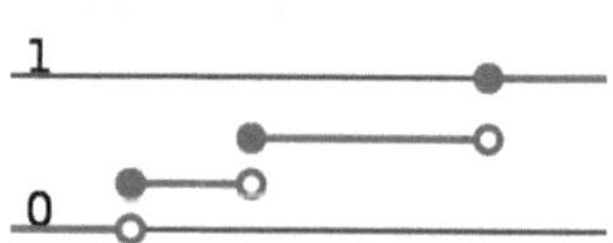

The cdf of a discrete probability distribution, ...

Cumulative density

Equivalently to the above, a discrete random variable can be defined as a random variable whose cumulative distribution function (cdf) increases only by jump discontinuities—that is, its cdf increases only where it "jumps" to a higher value, and is constant between those jumps. The points where jumps occur are precisely the values which

... of a continuous probability distribution, ...

the random variable may take. The number of such jumps may be finite or countably infinite. The set of locations of such jumps need not be topologically discrete; for example, the cdf might jump at each rational number.

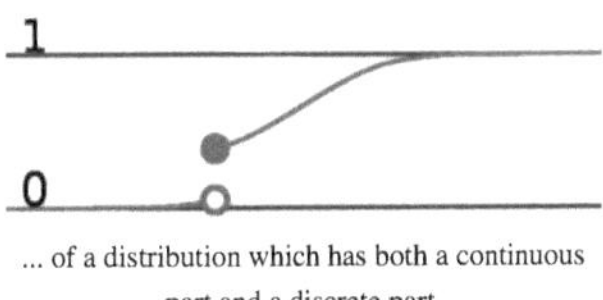

... of a distribution which has both a continuous part and a discrete part.

Delta-function representation

Consequently, a discrete probability distribution is often represented as a generalized probability density function involving Dirac delta functions, which substantially unifies the treatment of continuous and discrete distributions. This is especially useful when dealing with probability distributions involving both a continuous and a discrete part.

Indicator-function representation

For a discrete random variable X, let u_0, u_1, ... be the values it can take with non-zero probability. Denote

These are disjoint sets, and by formula (1)

It follows that the probability that X takes any value except for u_0, u_1, ... is zero, and thus one can write X as

except on a set of probability zero, where is the indicator function of A. This may serve as an alternative definition of discrete random variables.

Continuous probability distribution

A **continuous probability distribution** shall be understood as a *probability distribution* that has a probability density function. Mathematicians also call such a distribution **absolutely continuous**, since its cumulative distribution function is absolutely continuous with respect to the Lebesgue measure λ. If the distribution of X is continuous, then X is called a **continuous random variable**. There are many examples of continuous probability distributions: normal, uniform, chi-squared, and others.

Intuitively, a continuous random variable is the one which can take a continuous range of values — as opposed to a discrete distribution, where the set of possible values for the random variable is at most countable. While for a discrete distribution an event with probability zero is impossible (e.g. rolling 3½ on a standard die is impossible, and has probability zero), this is not so in the case of a continuous random variable. For example, if one measures the width of an oak leaf, the result of 3½ cm is possible, however it has probability zero because there are uncountably many other potential values even between 3 cm and 4 cm. Each of these individual outcomes has probability zero, yet the probability that the outcome will fall into the interval (3 cm, 4 cm) is nonzero. This apparent paradox is resolved by the fact that the probability that X attains some value within an infinite set, such as an interval, cannot be found by naively adding the probabilities for individual values. Formally, each value has an infinitesimally small probability, which statistically is equivalent to zero.

Formally, if X is a continuous random variable, then it has a probability density function $f(x)$, and therefore its probability of falling into a given interval, say $[a, b]$ is given by the integral

In particular, the probability for X to take any single value a (that is $a \le X \le a$) is zero, because an integral with coinciding upper and lower limits is always equal to zero.

The definition states that a continuous probability distribution must possess a density, or equivalently, its cumulative distribution function be absolutely continuous. This requirement is stronger than simple continuity of the cdf, and there is a special class of distributions, *singular distributions*, which are neither continuous nor discrete nor their mixture. An example is given by the Cantor distribution. Such singular distributions however are never encountered in practice.

Note on terminology: some authors use the term "continuous distribution" to denote the distribution with continuous cdf. Thus, their definition includes both the (absolutely) continuous and singular distributions.

By one convention, a probability distribution is called *continuous* if its cumulative distribution function is continuous and, therefore, the probability measure of singletons for all .

Another convention reserves the term *continuous probability distribution* for absolutely continuous distributions. These distributions can be characterized by a probability density function: a non-negative Lebesgue integrable function defined on the real numbers such that

Discrete distributions and some continuous distributions (like the Cantor distribution) do not admit such a density.

Probability distributions of real-valued random variables

Because a probability distribution Pr on the real line is determined by the probability of a real-valued random variable X being in a half-open interval $(-\infty, x]$, the probability distribution is completely characterized by its cumulative distribution function:

Terminology

The **support** of a distribution is the smallest closed interval/set whose complement has probability zero. It may be understood as the points or elements that are actual members of the distribution.

Some properties

- The probability density function of the sum of two independent random variables is the **convolution** of each of their density functions.
- The probability density function of the difference of two independent random variables is the **cross-correlation** of their density functions.
- Probability distributions are not a vector space – they are not closed under linear combinations, as these do not preserve non-negativity or total integral 1 – but they are closed under convex combination, thus forming a convex subset of the space of functions (or measures).

Random number generation

A frequent problem in statistical simulations (Monte Carlo method) is the generation of pseudo-random numbers that are distributed in a given way. Most algorithms are based on a pseudorandom number generator that produces numbers X that are uniformly distributed in the interval $[0,1)$. These X are then transformed to some $u(X)$ that satisfy a given distribution $f(u)$.

Kolmogorov definition

In the measure-theoretic formalization of probability theory, a random variable is defined as a measurable function X from a probability space to measurable space . A **probability distribution** is the pushforward measure $X_*P = PX^{-1}$ on .

Applications

The concept of the probability distribution and the random variables which they describe underlies the mathematical discipline of probability theory, and the science of statistics. There is spread or variability in almost any value that can be measured in a population (e.g. height of people, durability of a metal, sales growth, traffic flow, etc.); almost all measurements are made with some intrinsic error; in physics many processes are described probabilistically, from the kinetic properties of gases to the quantum mechanical description of fundamental particles. For these and many other reasons, simple numbers are often inadequate for describing a quantity, while probability distributions are often more appropriate.

As a more specific example of an application, the cache language models and other statistical language models used in natural language processing to assign probabilities to the occurrence of particular words and word sequences do so by means of probability distributions.

Common probability distributions

The following is a list of some of the most common probability distributions, grouped by the type of process that they are related to. For a more complete list, see list of probability distributions, which groups by the nature of the outcome being considered (discrete, continuous, multivariate, etc.)

Note also that all of the univariate distributions below are singly peaked; that is, it is assumed that the values cluster around a single point. In practice, actually observed quantities may cluster around multiple values. Such quantities can be modeled using a mixture distribution.

Related to real-valued quantities that grow linearly (e.g. errors, offsets)

- Normal distribution (Gaussian distribution), for a single such quantity; the most common continuous distribution

Related to positive real-valued quantities that grow exponentially (e.g. prices, incomes, populations)

- Log-normal distribution, for a single such quantity whose log is normally distributed
- Pareto distribution, for a single such quantity whose log is exponentially distributed; the prototypical power law distribution

Related to real-valued quantities that are assumed to be uniformly distributed over a (possibly unknown) region

- Discrete uniform distribution, for a finite set of values (e.g. the outcome of a fair die)
- Continuous uniform distribution, for continuously distributed values

Related to Bernoulli trials (yes/no events, with a given probability)

- Basic distributions:
  - Bernoulli distribution, for the outcome of a single Bernoulli trial (e.g. success/failure, yes/no)
  - Binomial distribution, for the number of "positive occurrences" (e.g. successes, yes votes, etc.) given a fixed total number of independent occurrences
  - Negative binomial distribution, for binomial-type observations but where the quantity of interest is the number of failures before a given number of successes occurs
  - Geometric distribution, for binomial-type observations but where the quantity of interest is the number of failures before the first success; a special case of the negative binomial distribution
- Related to sampling schemes over a finite population:
  - Hypergeometric distribution, for the number of "positive occurrences" (e.g. successes, yes votes, etc.) given a fixed number of total occurrences, using sampling without replacement
  - Beta-binomial distribution, for the number of "positive occurrences" (e.g. successes, yes votes, etc.) given a fixed number of total occurrences, sampling using a Polya urn scheme (in some sense, the "opposite" of sampling without replacement)

Related to categorical outcomes (events with K possible outcomes, with a given probability for each outcome)

- Categorical distribution, for a single categorical outcome (e.g. yes/no/maybe in a survey); a generalization of the Bernoulli distribution
- Multinomial distribution, for the number of each type of categorical outcome, given a fixed number of total outcomes; a generalization of the binomial distribution
- Multivariate hypergeometric distribution, similar to the multinomial distribution, but using sampling without replacement; a generalization of the hypergeometric distribution

Related to events in a Poisson process (events that occur independently with a given rate)

- Poisson distribution, for the number of occurrences of a Poisson-type event in a given period of time
- Exponential distribution, for the time before the next Poisson-type event occurs

Useful for hypothesis testing related to normally distributed outcomes

- Chi-squared distribution, the distribution of a sum of squared standard normal variables; useful e.g. for inference regarding the sample variance of normally distributed samples (see chi-squared test)
- Student's t distribution, the distribution of the ratio of a standard normal variable and the square root of a scaled chi squared variable; useful for inference regarding the mean of normally distributed samples with unknown variance (see Student's t-test)
- F-distribution, the distribution of the ratio of two scaled chi squared variables; useful e.g. for inferences that involve comparing variances or involving R-squared (the squared correlation coefficient)

Useful as conjugate prior distributions in Bayesian inference

- Beta distribution, for a single probability (real number between 0 and 1); conjugate to the Bernoulli distribution and binomial distribution
- Gamma distribution, for a non-negative scaling parameter; conjugate to the rate parameter of a Poisson distribution or exponential distribution, the precision (inverse variance) of a normal distribution, etc.
- Dirichlet distribution, for a vector of probabilities that must sum to 1; conjugate to the categorical distribution and multinomial distribution; generalization of the beta distribution
- Wishart distribution, for a symmetric non-negative definite matrix; conjugate to the inverse of the covariance matrix of a multivariate normal distribution; generalization of the gamma distribution

See also

- Moment-generating function
- Copula (statistics)
- Histogram
- Likelihood function
- List of statistical topics
- Riemann–Stieltjes integral application to probability theory

References

- B. S. Everitt: *The Cambridge Dictionary of Statistics*, Cambridge University Press, Cambridge (3rd edition, 2006). ISBN 0521690277
- Bishop: *Pattern Recognition and Machine Learning*, Springer, ISBN 0-387-31073-8

Article Sources and Contributors

Copying_mechanism *Source*: http://en.wikipedia.org/w/index.php?title=Copying_mechanism *Contributors*: David Eppstein, Eva kiszka, Grandsong, Infrangible, Michael Hardy, Oleg Alexandrov, Shreevatsa, Welsh, 4 anonymous edits

Scale-free_network *Source*: http://en.wikipedia.org/w/index.php?title=Scale-free_network *Contributors*: 3mta3, Agathman, Alexandersaschawolff, Andreala, Anville, Atddta, BarroColorado, Bobsponj, Brteag00, CesarB, ChaTo, Charles Matthews, Cheezycrust, ChrisGualtieri, Conradl, Cosmi, Cryoboy, DFRussia, Dandv, Danlev, DarwinPeacock, David Eppstein, DavidLevinson, Derlikous, Dirac1933, Dirkbb, Dlohcierekim, Dougher, Douglas R. White, Dratman, Dreftymac, Dwheeler, Echinoidea, Econterms, Edward, FlyingPenguins, Fmccown, Gareth McCaughan, Gmagkots, Gragus, Gritzko, Hannes Röst, Headbomb, Htmlism, Infoeco, JFromm, JimR, Joe Schmedley, JonDePlume, Jshadias, Kku, Kl4m, Kmote, Lethe, Longhair, MarkHudson, Massimo.franceschet, Mdd, Meekohi, Metasoarous, Michael Hardy, Miym, Mouse20080706, Myasuda, Nickg, Nog33, Octochimps, Oleg Alexandrov, Onlynone, PAR, PaulTanenbaum, Peak, Pphaneuf, RDBrown, Rjwilmsi, SanderSpek, Sandman2007, Smiling1126, T214OU, TedPavlic, Typochimp, Ugronugron, Ventania, WiseWoman, Yaronf, 140 anonymous edits

World_Wide_Web *Source*: http://en.wikipedia.org/w/index.php?title=World_Wide_Web *Contributors*: *feridiák, -Kerplunk-, 10metreh, 16@r, 194.109.232.xxx, 203.109.250.xxx, 20coconuts, 2206, 3rdTriangle, 5theye, 75th Trombone, 8ung3st, A Stop at Willoughby, ABF, AJR, AL3X TH3 GR8, AMHR285, AVand, Aamirbk1, AaronLLF, AaronTownsend, Abarry, Abatres, Abce2, Abd, Abdel.a.saleh, Abovemost, Abrech, Acather96, Accurizer, Acuppert, AdamXgamer, Adashiel, Adrian.benko, Aeolien, Aesopos, Af648, AgadaUrbanit, Ageekgal, Agendum, Agent Smith (The Matrix), Ahoerstemeier, Akendall, Al guy, Alan Liefting, Alansohn, AlefZet, Alerante, AlexWangombe, Alexf, Alexius08, Alexjohnc3, AlistairMcMillan, Alokchakrabarti, Alpha Quadrant (alt), Alphachimp, Alvestrand, Amillar, Amplitude101, AmyzzXX, Andre Engels, Andrea Parri, Andrew D. Jones, Android Mouse, Andromeda321, Andy Dingley, Andyjsmith, Angela, Anomalocaris, Anonymous Dissident, Anonymous101, Antandrus, Anthony, AntiVan, Aodonnel, Applechair, ArchonMagnus, Arensa, Argonistic professor, ArnoldReinhold, Arnon Chaffin, Art LaPella, Arthena, Artw, Aselfcallednowhere, Ash, Asteffey, Astrobloby, Atomice, Autopilots, Avono, Avram, Awanta, B, Balloomc, Bambuway, Bananaclaw, Barek, Barras, Barthandelus, Bbatsell, Bdesham, Beavis6325, Beddingplane, Beetstra, Beland, Bender235, Bendy1, Benqish, Bevo, Bgs264, Bibi Saint-Pol, Big Bird, BigHaz, BilCat, BillFlis, Billoraani123, Birds are weird, Bk0, Blacabyss, BlackAndy, Blahcake666, Bloodshedder, Bluffmaster541, Bo, Bo Lindbergh, Bobblewik, Bobet, Bobo192, Boccobrock, Boerman, Bongwarrior, Bookandcoffee, Bookofjude, Boomshadow, Boraxx, Boris Allen, Borislav, Boriszex, Bornhj, Bossk-Office, Bostonian Mike, Bounce1337, Branddobbe, Brian0918, Brianga, Brion VIBBER, Bronger, Brougham96, Bryan Derksen, Buchanan-Hermit, BudSipkiss, Buddyscruggs, BuffStuffer, Bumm13, Burto88, Butters77777, BziB, CSEditor, CUTKD, Cabbatime, Cadiomals, Cailliau, Calvin 1998, Camster342, Can't sleep, clown will eat me, Canadian-Bacon, CanadianLinuxUser, Capricorn42, CaptainVindaloo, CardinalDan, Carlsotr, Cenarium, Centrx, Charraksus, Chbarts, Chininazu12, Chip1990, Chris 73, Chris G, ChrisLoosley, Christian List, Christopher Parham, Chuckiesdad, CiaPan, Cielomobile, Cirrus Editor, Claidheamohmor, Classicfilms, Claud1996, CliffC, Clirmion, Closedmouth, Clpo13, Cntras, Coflo1994, Coldfire82, Colijunior, CommonsDelinker, Computerjoe, ComradeSlice, Connelly90, Conversion script, Coolcaesar, Cooldemilou, Coolninja98, Coplston, CoramN, Corpx, Correctingothers, Corvus cornix, Courcelles, Cov87, Cpbaseball5, CrazyChemGuy, Crazycomputers, Credema, Crisco 1492, Cst17, Cuahl, Cwolfsheep, Cybercobra, Cyclopia, Cyde, D, D6, DARTH SIDIOUS 2, DBigXray, DD2K, DJ Clayworth, DMacks, DRBar, DVdm, Daaah5, Daedelus, Damian Yerrick, Dan100, Dancter, Danny5000, DarkFalls, Darkenn, Darkwind, Darkx1337, Darth Panda, Dave6, Daveblack, Daverocks, Daverose 33, Daveydweeb, David Gerard, David Latapie, David Starkey, David.Mestel, DavidLevinson, Davnor, Davodd, Dawnseeker2000, Dbsanfte, DeadEyeArrow, DearPrudence, Deathtopudding, Decltype, Deepugn, Den fjättrade ankan, Denis C., Denisarona, DennyColt, DerHexer, DestroyerBDT, Diamond2, Diberri, Dickguertin, DigbyDalton, Dina, DirkvdM, Discospinster, Dispenser, Djavidan, Djg2006, Dlrohrer2003, DocWatson42, Docbug, Doggieman159, Dogmavskarma, Dominic, Donfbreed, Doradus, DoubleBlue, Doug A. Hole, Download, Dputig07, DragonHawk, Drbb01, Drcarver, DreamGuy, Drift chambers, DriveMySol, Drmies, Drphilharmonic, Drunken Pirate, Dry., Dube-k Nkiribari, DugDownDeep, Dustinasby, Dwilz, Dylan Damien, Dynaflow, Dzhatse, E Wing, EagleFan, Eagleamn, Eamonn sullivan, Eagleblrd, EarthPerson, Editmaniac, Edward Zimmermann, EdwinHJ, Efitu, Egmontaz, Ehsan™, El C, El0i, ElfQrin, Elmoro, Eloquence, Eluchil404, EmeryD, Emperorbma, Eneville, Enil, Epbr123, EpicBit, Erick.Antezana, Ericoides, Esanchez7587, Escalader, Everyking, Excirial, Exert, Eyu100, Freu, Falcai, FatalError, FeldBum, Fenrisulfr, Fireice, Flewis, Florentino floro, Flowerparty, Flowerpotman, Flyer 13, Fmccown, Foxwolfblood, Fratrep, Freakinginie, Freakofnurture, Frederik S, Ftu78, Fumitol, Func, Furrykef, G2g2day, GB fan, GDonato, Gail, Gaius Cornelius, Garion96, Gary King, Gary the gnome, Gary13579, Gdo01, Geniac, Genixp, Gholson, Giftlite, Giggy, Gilliam, GlassCobra, Glenn, Gman124, Gobonobo, Gogo Dodo, GoingBatty, Gooday.1, Goplat, Gott wisst, Gracenotes, GraemeL, Graham87, Grantglendinning, Grawity, Graylorde, Greatbigtwit, Grison, Gsandi, Gscshoyru, Gsklee, Gun Powder Ma, Guoguo12, Gurch, Gustav von Humpelschmumpel, Gwernol, H2g2bob, Hadal, Hailey C. Shannon, Hairy Dude, Ham123de, HamburgerRadio, Happy darrenchong, Hardyplants, Harfi66, Harmil, Harryboyles, Harryzilber, Haseo9999, Hashar, Hassim1983, Headbomb, Hellisp, Hendry, Henry Flower, Herehere, HexaChord, HiJohnSpencer, Highonhendrix, Hillgentleman, Hon-3s-T, Hoof Hearted, Hotcrocodile, Howdoesthiswo, Hrvoje Simic, Hugovanmeijeren, Hung3rd, Husond, Huw Powell, Hydrogen Iodide, I amm Beowulf!, I dream of horses, IByte, II MusLiM HyBRiD II, IMSoP, IRP, IShadowed, IW.HG, Icairns, Icrutt, Ignatzmice, Imgaril, Imnotminkus, Informatic17, Inoen, Inter, Invistec, Ipso2, Iridescent, Ironrd, Irrbloss, Isam, Isilanes, Ixfd64, J.delanoy, JFG, JForget, JHMM13, JNW, Ja2k8el, Jackol, JacobCurtis, Jacobolus, Jake Wartenberg, Jake-515-, JamesBWatson, Jamie89104, Jasper Deng, Jatkins, Javidan, Jayhawk of Justice, Jblatt, Jedsayaman, Jeff G., Jeffq, Jeffreylkk, Jehfes, Jeltz, Jengod, JeremyA, Jeveteca, Jfdwolff, Jhessela, JialiangGao, Jim1138, Jimmi Hugh, Jj137, Jjshapiro, Jleedev, Jmfriesen, Jnc, Jncraton, Jneal55, Joanjoc, Joe11miles, JoeOnSunset, Joeblakesley, JohanL, John, John Broughton, John Carter, John Fader, Johnl, JohnOwens, JohnPritchard, JohnTechnologist, Johnwrw, JokelineUK, JonHarder, Jonathan Drain, Jonvvv2, JordeeBec, Jorel1314, Jorunn, Joseph Solis in Australia, Josephf, Joshthegreat, Joshua, Joshua Issac, Josquius, Jovianeye, Joy, Jpbowen, Jpo, Jrockley, Jsmestad, Jtiza, Jufert, Jugander, Juliancolton, Junnel, Junon, Jusdafax, Justinfr, JzG, Jzylstra, KYPark, Kaiyir Minoia, Karen Johnson, Karl Stas, Karlson2k, Karmona, Kate, Katieh5584, Kbolino, Kbrose, Keilana, Kenny sh, Kezze, Khalid, Kim Bruning, Kingsaini, Kirbytime, Kiwi128, KiwiRyan, Kkram, Knff, Knutux, Koavf, Korath, Korg, Kornfan71, Kpwa gok, KrakatoaKatie, Krishvanth, Krothor, Kubigula, KuroiShiroi, Kvasilev, Kvng, Kwamikagami, Kwiki, Kwlothrop, Kyle1278, L Kensington, LUUSAP, Lachatdelarue, Lakefall, Lars Trebing, Lars Washington, Ldg2135a-14, Leafyplant, Leandrod, Learnaffilate, Lee Carre, Lee Daniel Crocker, Lee S. Svoboda, Legedevin, Leonig Mig, Leszek Jańczuk, Letdorf, Levineps, Lifefeed, Lightmouse, Ligulem, Little Mountain 5, LittleOldMe, LizardJr8, Loalhe, Logan, Loki500, Longhair, LorenzoB, Lotje, Lovetinkle, Lowellian, Luk, Luna Santin, Lwoodyiii, Lykoyrgos, Lynchyboi, MBisanz, MC10, MER-C, MITBeaverRocks, MONGO, Mabdul, Mac, Macy, Maestrosync, Magicxcian, Mail4james, Mailer diablo, Malatesta, Malcolm Farmer, Malleus Fatuorum, Manbilong, Manop, Manway, Marek69, Mark Arsten, Mark Foskey, Mark91, Markaci, Mars fenix, Martinp, Master Jay, Master of Puppets, Masterhomer, Matt Gies, Matt McIrvin, Matt Yeager, MattGiuca, Matteh, Matthieupinard, Mattisse, Matusz, Maurreen, Mav, Maxamegalon2000, Maxis ftw, Maxschmelling, Mayooranathan, Mayor Westfall, Mbell, McSly, Mcalliph, Mcm, Mdbest, Mditto, Meigwil, Mentifisto, Meowkittymeow, Mervyn, Meshach, Metao, Mets501, Mgiganteus1, Michael Hardy, MichaelJanich, Michaeljr97, Michaeloqu, MikeWren, Mindmatrix, Minghong, Mini-Geek, Minimac, Mirt Tenk, MisterCharlie, Mjb, Mjgw, Mlouns, Modemac, Mohitngm, Monty845, Moogwrench, Mooquackwooftweetmeow, Moriori, Mort432, Mr random, Mr. Lefty, Mrqueen, Mrzaius, Mschel, Msikma, Mttcmbs, Mumia-w-18, Musicandnintendo, Muso799, Mvuijlst, Mxn, My favourite teddy bear, Mywyb2, NCurse, NEO369, NHRHS2010, Naerii, Nageh, Nagy, Nakon, Nanshu, NantonosAedui, Nantoseiken, Nathanlandis, NawlinWiki, Nbarth, NeilN, Nepenthes, Nertzy, Netoholic, Netvor, Neutral current, Neutrino007, NewEnglandYankee, Newmac, Newmanbe, Nicholasstorriearce, Nick C, NickBush24, Nigelj, Nihiltres, Nikai, Nishkid64, Nivix, Nixeagle, Nkeel34, Nlu, Noah Salzman, Noformation, Noisy, Noldoaran, NorthernThunder, Not home, NotinREALITY, Nubiatech, Nurg, Oberst, Oblivious, Qf, Ohnoitsjamie, Ohsayanything, Okiefromokla, Olgerd, Oli Filth, Oliver Pereira, Olivier Debre, OnePt618, Oniscoid, Onorem, Open4D, Orange Suede Sofa, Orderinchaos, OregonD00d, Oroso, Ost316, Ours, Outriggr, OverlordQ, Oxymoron83, Paliku, Pastore Italy, Patelmihirb, Patrick, Paul Ebermann, PaulGarner, Pedxing385, Pemboid, Persian Poet Gal, Peter Campbell, Peter Karlsen, Petrb, Petskratt, Pgan002, Phact, PhantomS, Pharaoh of the Wizards, Phil Boswell, PhilKnight, Philip Trueman, Phoenix Hacker, Piano non troppo, Picturesofmia, Pigsonthewing, Pinethicket, Pinkadelica, Pintopc, Pnm, Porqin, Possum, Postlewaight, Poulpy, Poweroid, Ppk01, Ppp, Prender101, Prenn, PrestonH, Prestonmcconkie, Pretty Green, Prezbo, Proofreader, PseudoSudo, Psy guy, Publicly Visible, Putanginanyo, Pyrolord747, Pádraic MacUidhir, Qmt, Quebec99, QuiteUnusual, Qwanqwa, Qwerty0, Qwyrxian, Qxz, RJaguar3, RUL3R, Radar scanner, RadioActive, Radu Gherasim, Raeky, Ragesoss, Rainbow sprinkle, RainbowOfLight, Raining girl, Rama, RandomP, Randomreturn, Rannpháirtí anaithnid, Rasmus Faber, Rathfalguni, Raul654, Rav77, Raven in Orbit, Rawr, Razor 69, Razorflame, Rbellin, Rbrwr, Reaper Eternal, Recognizance, Redl D Oon, RedWolf, Redtroll, ReeceSpielman, Remember the dot, RememberSammyJankis, Reneeholle, Res2216firestar, Rettetast, Rex1637, RexNL, Rhondalorraine, Rhopkins8, Rich Farmbrough, RichardF, RickK, Rjensen, Rjwilmsi, Rmccue, Roadrunner, Robert4668, RobertG, Robertvan1, Robomanx, RockMFR, Rompe, Ronhjones, Ronkronk, Ronny8, Ronz, RossPatterson, Rrburke, Rrfayette, Ruch37, Rws591, Ryan Postlethwaite, Ryan Roos, RyanGerbil10, Ryguillian, Ryulong, S.K., S8333631, SDC, SGBailey, SNIyer12, SQL, ST47, Sabariganesh, Saebjorn, Sam Korn, Samwb123, Sander Säde, Sango123, SasiSasi, Satori Son, Savidan, Sbrentegani, Scalkin, Scandum, Scartboy, SchuminWeb, Schweiwikist, Scohoust, Scottyhoohow, Sean William, Seaphoto, Securityadvisor, Seedat, Septagram, Seraphim, Sesshomaru, Seth Ilys, Sh4rk4tt4ck, Shanimoshe, Shantavira, Sharon08tam, Shii, Shirik, Shot, Shotwell, Siebrand, Simbu123, Simetrical, SimonD, Sionus, Siteshwar, Sjh, Sjjupadhyay, Sjmtlewy, Skeejay, Skierpage, Skizzik, Sky Attacker, SkyMachine, Sligocki, Sliker Hawk, Slovakia, Smalljim, Snakekiller1x95, Snarl, Solidsandie, Someguy1221, Someone else, Sonjaaa, SpNeo, Spam kj, SpeakFree, Specs112, Speer320, Spitfire19, Splarka, SpuriousQ, Ssolbergj, Staeiou, Staticfree, Stbalbach, Stephan Leeds, Stephen Walling, Steven Weston, Steven Zhang, Stirling Newberry, Strait, Sue Anne, Suffusion of Yellow, Sugarbeartrio, Sundar, Sunkorg, Sunray, Superm401, Supten, Surfingslovak, SusanLesch, Susokukan47, Susurrus, Swatje, SweetNeo85, Symane, Synthe, Syrthiss, T3chl0v3r, TMC, Ta bu shi da yu, Tangotango, TarkanAttila, TarmoK, Tarquin, Tbhotch, Tbutzon, Tcncv, Technopat, Teles, Tellyaddict, Tempshill, TenOfAllTrades, Teravolt, Tfmb, Tgeairn, That Guy, From That Show!, ThatWikiGuy, The Anome, The Evil IP address, The JPS, The Man in Question, The Rambling Man, The Random Editor, The Thing That Should Not Be, The Utahraptor, The monkeyhate, The sock that should not be, The sunder king, TheDevilOnLine, TheNoise, TheRhani, Theblackplague, Theraven, Theskitone, Thespian, Thingg, Thinktdub, Thomas For., Thrustinj, Thue, Thundercross16, Tide rolls, TimTomTom, Timbl, Timlane, Timmywimmy, Timrollpickering, Timwi, Tiptoety, Tiramisoo, Tobby72, Tobias Bergemann, Tommarsh99, Tomos, Tony1, Torgo, Tothwolf, Towel401, Tpbradbury, Trakesht, Travis99, Tregoweth, Trenchcoatjedi, Trialsanderrors, Troy 07, True Scaffold, Tsmith189, Ttwo1101, TuukkaH, Twang, Twinsday, Twobells, Tyciol, Tyw7, UA1high, UBeR, UU, UberScienceNerd, Ukulele, Ulmanor, Ultimus, Uman, Uncle Dick, Uncle Milty, Unreal7, Unyoyega, UpstateNYer, Uriah923, Useight, Usergreatpower, Utcursch, VMS Mosaic, VanBurenen, Vanished user 03, Venera Seyranyan, Verne Equinox, Versageek, Viajero, Vicoar, Villafanuk, Virii, Vishnava, Vladkornea, VolatileChemical, Vrenator, Vycanis, W3forum, WDGraham, Wacco, Waggers, Wanderingstan, Wang ty87916, Wangi, Wasssupman2000, Wavelength, Web mbaven, Weevil, Wertydm, Weyes, Whazzit, Wikibofh, Wikid77, Wikideman, Wikieditor06, Wikifun95, Wikimalta, Wikimancer, Wikipelli, Wildman7856, William Avery, Willking1979, Willsey1997, Wimt, Windharp, Wireless Keyboard, Wizofaus, Wknight94, Woody, Woohookitty, Wrinehart, Wsxx, Wtmitchell, Wwwwolf, XXBassmanXx, Xdenizen, Xezbeth, Xithen, Yacht, Yama, Yamla, YellowMonkey, Yemal, Yizhenwilliam, Yoelper, Yori, Yvesnimmo, Z3ugmatic, Zaf, Zaq12wsx, Zealotgi, Zenohockey, Zhente, ZimZalaBim, Zondor, Zoney, Zundark, Zzuuzz, , 2466 anonymous edits

Preferential_attachment *Source*: http://en.wikipedia.org/w/index.php?title=Preferential_attachment *Contributors*: AnAj, Auntof6, Avenue, Babbage, BarroColorado, Fheyligh, Headbomb, Janlo, Joe Decker, Loodog, Mandarax, Melcombe, Meok, Michael Hardy, Nbarth, Nog33, Oleg Alexandrov, Omnipaedista, PAR, Rjwilmsi, Tsirel, 8 anonymous edits

Degree_distribution *Source*: http://en.wikipedia.org/w/index.php?title=Degree_distribution *Contributors*: AnAj, Athenray, Bpringlemeir, Btyner, Cannibaltinea, Charles Matthews, Gritzko, Headbomb, Kku, MarkSweep, Meekohi, Michael Slone, Nog33, Rjwilmsi, Sam Blacketer, Scrisostomo, Taxipom, Wuyilin, 13 anonymous edits

Power_law *Source*: http://en.wikipedia.org/w/index.php?title=Power_law *Contributors*: 16@r, 213.253.39.xxx, Agl, Akadruid, Andycjp, Antonielly, Athkalani, BlaiseFEgan, Bobblewik, Canalyst, CecilWard, Chemical Engineer, Ciemo, Ciencias69, Clementi, Conversion script, Cyberman, DPoisson, DaveApter, DeFaultRyan, Derek farn, DerekLaw, Dicklyon, Dougher, Dsornette, ElectricRay, Eurobas, Experiment123, Faradayplank, Fentlehan, Fpahl, Gaborgulya, Gap9551, Giftlite, Gymnotus, Headbomb, Hedkace, Heron, Igitur, Ikip, JA(000)Davidson, Jcegobrain, JerzyTarasiuk, JimR, JoaoMenezes, Jrtayloriv, Karada, Kelisi, Kku, KnightRider, Kolmogorov Complexity, Kwantus, Lexor, Locke'sGhost, Loodog, Maitchy, Maltusnet, Math.geek3.1415926, Melcombe, Mfloryan, Michael Hardy, Mild Bill Hiccup, Mindmatrix, Mompox, Mtyrone, MuDavid, Mythobeast, Nbarth, Niceguyedc, Nichtich, Nickj, Ninly, Nog33, NonNobis, Nugecom, Octochimps, Olin, Ott2, Paintitblack ft, Paresnah, Pcb21, Pelex, Poor Yorick, Ptery, Ptrf, Quaeler, Reedy, Rhetth, Rjwilmsi, Skippy le Grand Gourou, Smack, Steven Walling, Stevep001, Structuralgeol, Sundar, Tarquin, The Anome, TheLastWordSword, Themel, Thumperward, Thurth, Thw1, Ugronugron, Uncle G, Urdutext, Waldir, WebDrake, Wellithy, WhiteHatLurker, Wragge, Xykatra, Yocto12, ZeroOne, Zosoin, Zuckyd1, 134 anonymous edits

Probability_distribution *Source*: http://en.wikipedia.org/w/index.php?title=Probability_distribution *Contributors*: (:Julien:), 198.144.199.xxx, 3mta3, A.M.R., A5, Abhinav316, AbsolutDan, Adrokin, Alansohn, Alexius08, Amircrypto, Ap, Applepiein, Avenue, AxelBoldt, BD2412, Baccyak4H, Benwing, Bfigura's puppy, Bhoola Pakistani, Bkkbrad, Branny 96, Bryan Derksen, Btyner, Calvin 1998, Caramdir, Cburnett, Chirlu, Chris the speller, Classical geographer, Closedmouth, Conversion script, Courcelles, Csigabi, Damian Yerrick, Davhorn, David Eppstein, David Vose, DavidCBryant, Dcljr, Delldot, Den fjättrade ankan, Dick Beldin, Digisus, Dino, Domminico, Dysprosia, Eliezg, Emijrp, Epbr123, Eric Kvaalen, Fintor, Firelog, Fnielsen, Frietjes, G716, Gaius Cornelius, Gala.martin, Gandalf61, Gate2quality, Giftlite, Gjnyasa, GoodDamon, Graham87, Hamamelis, Hu12, Hughperkins, I dream of horses, ImperfectlyInformed, It Is Me Here, Iwaterpolo, J.delanoy, JJ Harrison, JRSpriggs, Jan eissfeldt, JayJasper, Jclemens, Jipumarino, Jitse Niesen, Jncraton, Johndburger, Jojalozzo, Jon Awbrey, Josuechan, Jsd115, Jsnx, Jtkiefer, Kastchei, Knutux, Larryisgood, LiDaobing, Lilac Soul, Lollerskates, Lotje, Loupeter, MGriebe, Magioladitis, Marie Poise, MarkSweep, Markhebner, Marner, Megaloxantha, Melcombe, Mental Blank, Michael Hardy, Miguel, MisterSheik, Morton.lin, MrOllie, Napzilla, Nbarth, NuclearWarfare, O18, OdedSchramm, Ojigiri, OlEnglish, OverInsured, Oxymoron83, PAR, Pabristow, Patrick, Paul August, Pax:Vobiscum, Pgan002, Phys, Ponnu, Poor Yorick, Populus, Ptrf, Quietbritishjim, Qwfp, Riceplaytexas, Rich Farmbrough, Richard D. LeCour, Rinconsoleao, Roger.simmons, Rumping, Rursus, Salgueiro, Salix alba, Samois98, Sandym, Schmock, Seglea, Serguei S. Dukachev, ServiceAT, ShaunES, Shizhao, Silly rabbit, SiobhanHansa, Sky Attacker, Statlearn, Stpasha, TNARasslin, TakuyaMurata, Tarotcards, Tayste, Techman224, Tedtoal, TexasDawg, Thamelry, The Anome, The Thing That Should Not Be, TheCoffee, Tillander, Tomi, Topology Expert, Tordek ar, Tsirel, Ttony21, Unyoyega, Uvainio, Velella, VictorAnyakin, WestwoodMatt, Whosasking, Whosyourjudas, X-Bert, Xuhuyang, Zundark, 265 anonymous edits

Image Sources, Licenses and Contributors

Printed by Books on Demand GmbH, Norderstedt / Germany